I0802188

* * * * * * *

"Skin picking, hair pulling, and other BFRBs can feel isolating and hard to change. This workbook gives teens and young adults clear explanations, practical tools, and step-by-step strategies to build awareness, create new habits, and make lasting progress."

—**Katie K. May,** LPC, Founder of Creative Healing Teen Support Centers

* * * * * * *

"This practical workbook offers 'you got this' support for teens and young adults with BFRBs, guiding them through a 10-week program to set intentions, build awareness, seek appropriate support, and identify intervention strategies to gain confidence on their road to recovery."

—**Dr Renae Reinardy,** co-author of *The BFRB Recovery Workbook*

* * * * * * *

The BFRB Workbook for Teens and Young Adults

of related interest

The BFRB Recovery Workbook
Effective Recovery from Hair Pulling, Skin Picking, Nail Biting, and Other Body-Focused Repetitive Behaviors
Marla W. Deibler, PsyD, ABPP and Renae M. Reinardy, PsyD
ISBN 978 1 83997 655 1
eISBN 978 1 83997 656 8

The ADHD Teen Survival Guide
Your Launchpad to an Amazing Life
Soli Lazarus
Designed and illustrated by Kara McHale
ISBN 978 1 83997 663 6
eISBN 978 1 83997 664 3

The Anxiety Recovery Journal
Creative Activities to Keep Yourself Well
Cara Lisette and Anneli Roberts
Illustrated by Victoria Barron
Foreword by Annie Hickox
ISBN 978 1 80501 079 1
eISBN 978 1 80501 080 7
Creative Journals for Mental Health

My Anxiety Handbook
Getting Back on Track
Sue Knowles, Bridie Gallagher and Phoebe McEwen
Illustrated by Emmeline Pidgen
ISBN 978 1 78592 440 8
eISBN 978 1 78450 813 5
Handbooks Series

The BFRB Workbook for Teens and Young Adults

Recover from Skin Picking, Hair Pulling, and other Body-Focused Repetitive Behaviors

Dr Laura Chackes

with **Lauren McKeaney** of
The Picking Me Foundation

Jessica Kingsley Publishers
London and Philadelphia

First published in Great Britain in 2026 by Jessica Kingsley Publishers
An imprint of John Murray Press

1

A CIP catalogue record for this title is available from the British Library and the Library of Congress

ISBN 978 1 80501 865 0
eISBN 978 1 80501 866 7

Printed and bound in Great Britain by Bell & Bain Limited

Jessica Kingsley Publishers' policy is to use papers that are natural, renewable and recyclable products and made from wood grown in sustainable forests. The logging and manufacturing processes are expected to conform to the environmental regulations of the country of origin.

Jessica Kingsley Publishers
Carmelite House
50 Victoria Embankment
London EC4Y 0DZ

www.jkp.com

John Murray Press
Part of Hodder & Stoughton Ltd
An Hachette Company

The authorized representative in the EEA is Hachette Ireland, 8 Castlecourt Centre, Dublin 15, D15 XTP3, Ireland (email: info@hbgi.ie)

Table of Contents

Acknowledgments

LAURA

I would like to thank Kara Friedman, LPC, for editing this book and helping to give it an authentic teen voice. Her willingness to help and enthusiasm for the project encouraged me throughout the entire process.

Thank you to Alec Pollard, PhD, for selecting me for the postdoctoral fellowship at St. Louis Behavioral Medicine Institute (SLBMI) in 2005, which sparked my passion for treating OCD, and for then suggesting that I become an expert in trichotillomania. Little did I know that moment would lead to a career centered on this specialty, and that I'd become the leading BFRB expert in the entire St. Louis area, and one of the leading BFRB experts in the world.

Thank you to Lauren McKeaney for being one of the first to show me what recovery from a BFRB looks like, something she so beautifully portrays in this book. I'm grateful for your decades of collaboration and the ongoing motivation to keep sharing our knowledge and experience in new and meaningful ways.

Thank you to my husband and kids, Barry, Parker, and Liviya Tonopolsky, for your patience, love, and support, even when I am not around much due to the demands of this work.

And finally, thank you to my parents, Ken and Carole Chackes, for your unwavering encouragement to keep reaching for my dreams and the pride you show when I do.

LAUREN

I would like to thank my dad, F. Owen McKeaney, for making me believe in my voice. He always encouraged me to write and speak, and I know he would be proud of me and my published work today.

Thank you to Laura Chackes for our ongoing, collaborative, and inspiring relationship, personally and professionally, and for trusting my experience and guidance with this book.

To the Picking Me Foundation, the only nonprofit dedicated solely to skin picking disorder, thank you for helping my purpose pick me.

And to my fellow skin pickers, your journeys are valid, valuable, and worthy of being told. Thank you for being part of our powerful and empowering community. I am forever grateful for you.

Introduction

I don't have a BFRB myself, but I have struggled with anxiety throughout my life. I was so anxious that I didn't speak at all in preschool. Not one single time. So I started therapy at the age of three, and although I didn't speak to my therapist for the first year or so, I eventually overcame that fear and began speaking in school. My anxiety didn't totally go away, but over the years I learned how to manage it.

I graduated high school and went away to college, still feeling shy but a little more confident because I had my best friend by my side. After college, I went straight into grad school, where I had to push myself even harder to regularly participate in class in order to succeed. Now in my career as a psychologist, I've been able to speak in front of large crowds of people. I'm always still nervous at first, but when I'm talking about something I'm passionate about, like treatments for Body-Focused Repetitive Behaviors (BFRBs) that really work, I'm able to find my voice and speak confidently to hundreds of people. I will still be anxious at times, but it doesn't rule my life anymore.

Soon after I began treating BFRBs in 2006, I learned that treatment for these disorders was not very effective. At that time, the very limited research on trichotillomania (hair pulling—the first BFRB to be added to the manual we use to diagnose psychiatric conditions) showed that only about 10% of those who went through treatment recovered from the disorder. I was also treating severe obsessive compulsive disorder (OCD) at the time in an intensive outpatient program (IOP) and was seeing around 80% of my OCD patients reaching recovery. I couldn't understand why there'd be such a big difference between these similar disorders.

When I first started working with people who struggled with hair pulling and skin picking, I kept hearing the same thing over and over: "I must be the only person who does this." My patients felt intense shame, convinced that no one else in the world could possibly understand what they were going through.

I found myself saying again and again that they weren't alone—I wished I could introduce them to each other so they could see for themselves.

That's when I got the idea to start my first BFRB therapy group. I created separate groups for adults, teens, and kids, and right away, something amazing happened. From the very first session, I saw the shame and isolation start to disappear. There were even moments when people cried—not out of sadness but because they'd finally realized—I'm not the only one who does this. They met others who pulled or picked just like them, and suddenly, they didn't feel like "freaks" or "crazy" anymore. They began to understand that these behaviors didn't define them or make them bad people, and this then allowed them to finally start learning ways to manage their behaviors.

Over the past 18 years, I've refined this approach into a 10-week online group program that combines science-backed treatments with a supportive community. It's been incredible to see how effective this has been—people who stick with it experience real improvement, and even better, they keep those gains over time. Now, we're even studying this approach at UCLA to officially measure how well it works. But I already know from experience: it does.

One of the amazing people with a BFRB I met in one of my first groups was Lauren McKeaney. Upon meeting Lauren, I immediately noticed something different about her. Lauren wasn't afraid to spread awareness about BFRBs by sharing her personal story of having dermatillomania (aka skin picking disorder). And her ability, curiosity, and willingness to take on, process, and work through her experience was unique. Lauren's skin picking story wasn't an easy one to tell. From losing hours a day picking to numerous infection-driven hospital stays, Lauren really suffered with her BFRB. She felt alone in her community, misunderstood by her family, and unable to gain control of her skin picking.

Through the years, watching Lauren take control of her BFRB, and dedicating her career to advocacy, education, and awareness of skin picking disorder, has been incredibly impressive. Her courage and strength to fight through the shame and embarrassment that these disorders often cause, sharing with the world what it's authentically like to have a BFRB, is in large part so that other young people won't have to live with a secret like she did for so many years.

When Lauren first shared about her BFRB, empowered with a diagnosis and understanding of what she had, she knew she wanted others to feel the freedom she finally felt. Starting the hashtag #PickingMe, Lauren began conversations around her skin picking on social media, leading to almost 10,000 others joining the conversation. She knew she wanted to do something for her people, creating the home, the foundation, she had always been looking for.

In 2016, Lauren started the only 501(c)(3) nonprofit dedicated to skin picking disorder, the Picking Me Foundation, which has made a huge impact by offering hope, help, and healing to skin pickers and their loved ones alike. Plus, she is spreading awareness and inspiring acceptance by educating dermatologists, mental health professionals, and others who help those who suffer from dermatillomania know how to best work with and help her community. She is changing the narrative for skin pickers of all ages, helping them choose themselves over what chose them, #PickingMe over skin picking.

Lauren has become the foremost public speaker on skin picking disorder, speaking on her lived experience and the management strategies she has developed at over 200 occasions. Her story and work have been covered on VICE, in Vogue, and at international conferences worldwide. She runs the largest online skin picking support group, which has had over 5,500 attendees. To connect with her further, join her newsletter at https://pickingme.org/emailsignup or follow her across social media @laurenmckeaney.

Lauren and I have worked together in many capacities, from presenting to mental health professionals at international conferences to speaking to groups of BFRB sufferers in intimate online fireside chats. We enjoy each other personally and recommend each other professionally. When I started writing this book, I knew that Lauren had to be a part of it, as she has been an integral part of my professional journey. By sharing her personal skin picking stories from her teen and young adult years living with dermatillomania, along with her expert management advice, she will help you see what suffering and recovery look like from someone who has actually been through it. I hope you will find her stories as inspirational as I have found her and her foundation's work to be.

I'm excited to introduce this approach to a teen and young adult audience with this workbook. I know that a lot of teens and young adults aren't super into the idea of group therapy (trust me, I get it). But my hope is that this book gives you a way to build your own support system—whether that's friends, family, or even an online community—so you don't have to go through this alone.

This isn't just another boring self-help book. It's packed with creative and science-backed tools, along with Lauren's stories, so I think you might actually enjoy working through this (yes, really!). The best part? You'll see real progress. I've worked with so many people who have felt stuck for years, and when they finally start to feel better, they're beyond grateful. You deserve that feeling too. And with the right tools and support, you can absolutely get there.

Ready to get started?! It's totally normal to feel unsure about whether this will work for you, or even scared to get started. But if you don't give it a try, you'll never know. My best advice is to just get started and try not to focus on the outcome. You will definitely learn a lot, and even if you decide that you're not ready to focus on reducing the behavior, you will have developed a solid support system to help you navigate any life struggles. Part One of the book will teach you more about BFRBs in general, as well as your specific behaviors and feelings. Part Two will get you prepared for the work you're going to do. Part Three will give you specific steps to complete each week for 10 weeks. Throughout the workbook, you'll find practices and resources that you can download by visiting www.jkp.com/catalogue/book/9781805018650 or scanning the QR code below.

If you end up getting all the way through the workbook, you will have tools to manage not only your BFRB but also your thoughts and feelings about other stressors in your life. So it's really a win-win as long as you get started! I'm proud of you for just picking up this book and starting to read. You've got this!

PART ONE

LEARNING ABOUT MY BFRB

- CHAPTER 1 -

ABCDEFG... BFRB Say What?

PUTTING PIECES TOGETHER

Growing up, I lost hours a day compulsively picking my skin. I'd usually be stuck at a mirror trying to fix some perceived imperfection, likely until my hands cramped up and gave out from all the squeezing and scraping. It was exhausting.

Parents, doctors, teachers, friends, and others frustratingly told me to "Just stop picking!" (as if it were that simple). I longed to, with every pock-marked part of me. But nothing, no matter what I tried, seemed to help me stop picking. I felt mentally and physically torn apart. Broken. And unfixable.

For 27 years, I went undiagnosed and misdiagnosed. I was (incorrectly) told I had atopic dermatitis, eczema, sensitive skin, skin allergies, severe acne, and that I was self-harming.

None of this was true.

Medical experts and doctors said that I'd grow out of my compulsive skin picking, that I should try harder, and if I really wanted to stop, I would. None of that helped. I remained riddled with sores and shame.

It wasn't until the recognition of Body-Focused Repetitive Behaviors (BFRBs) in the DSM-5 (2013), the big, black book of mental illness, that I learned of this mental illness and received a diagnosis in 2014.

Having a name, a diagnosable medical disorder, for what I thought was just my brokenness, helped me feel whole.

And less alone.

The validation it offered empowered me, allowing me to actually start living my life.

Now, I like to say that I have it—it doesn't have me.

Lauren McKeaney

Did you know that 1 in 20 people have a BFRB? You are not alone! Most people who suffer from a BFRB don't even know that there is a name for what they do. If you ask a random person what a BFRB is, they will likely look at you with a blank look on their face. This is definitely a situation of IYKYK (if you know you know)! Incredibly, even lots of therapists don't know what a BFRB is.

HERE ARE SOME BASICS FOR YOU!

- BFRB stands for Body-Focused Repetitive Behavior. BFRBs are psychological disorders that cause people to pull out their hair, pick their skin, bite their nails, or repeatedly damage their body in some other way. Most people with BFRBs desperately want to stop the behavior; yet, at the same time, they often find that the behavior feels good—like scratching an itch.
- BFRBs can be different for different people. They are less severe for some, while for others it can be a really challenging and embarrassing part of their lives. As you may know, BFRBs can cause major damage to the hair or skin, like big bald spots on the scalp, missing eyelashes, or scabs and scars all over the body.
- The hair loss and marks on the skin often make the person with a BFRB feel intense embarrassment and shame, which often leads to them going to great lengths to cover up or hide the effects of their behavior. This can be especially hard if you already feel very concerned about your physical appearance, which is so common during this time of your life.

WHAT TYPES OF BFRBS DO YOU HAVE?

There are many different types of BFRBs. The most common ones are listed below. Put a checkmark next to any of the behaviors that are a problem for you. Don't worry if you have more than one of these; it's very common!

- ☐ **Skin picking disorder** (also known as excoriation disorder or dermatillomania): Excessive picking of the skin on your face or body (more than just popping a pimple) that takes up a lot of your time and/or causes significant damage to your skin.
- ☐ **Hair pulling disorder** (also known as trichotillomania): Repeated pulling of hair from your scalp, eyelashes, eyebrows, or any other body part that takes up a lot of your time and/or causes you to have bald spots or missing lashes or brows.

- ☐ **Nail biting** (also known as onychophagia): Repeated biting of your finger or toenails that causes excessive damage to your nails or surrounding skin.
- ☐ **Nail picking** (also known as onychotillomania): Repeated picking of your finger or toenails that causes excessive damage to your nails or surrounding skin.
- ☐ **Cheek biting** (also known as cheek keratosis): Repeated biting of the cheeks that causes sores in your mouth.
- ☐ **Lip biting** (also known as lip bite keratosis): Repeated biting of the lips that causes damage to your lips.
- ☐ **Tongue chewing**: Repeated biting of the tongue that causes damage to your tongue.
- ☐ **Nose picking** (also known as rhinotillexomania): Repeated picking of your nose that causes sores in your nose.
- ☐ **Skin biting** (also known as dermatophagia): Biting the cuticles, fingers, or skin on another part of your body, or eating scabs or skin (usually as a result of skin picking disorder).
- ☐ **Hair eating** (also known as trichophagia): May occur with hair pulling disorder when you chew on and then swallow the hair that you've pulled out.
- ☐ **Hair cutting** (also known as trichotemnomania): Repeated cutting of your hair.

HOW SEVERE IS YOUR BFRB?

In order to be officially called a disorder, the behavior must cause significant damage to your skin, hair, or other body part, cause significant distress, and/or disrupt your functioning in some way. Examples of disruption in functioning are spending too much time on it so that it gets in the way of you doing other things, or missing a party because you don't like how the picking or pulling made you look. However, the severity of BFRBs can range from mild to severe.

Use a marker to color in the boxes of each of the symptoms that sound like you to determine how severe your BFRB is.

Mild	Moderate	Severe
You pick at mosquito bites or acne, causing a few scabs on your face or body	You pick or bite your skin, nails, cheeks, or lips so often that you have noticeable scabs in multiple spots on your face or body	You have open wounds on your skin that won't heal because you can't stop picking them and/or you have scars all over your face or body

cont.

Mild	Moderate	Severe
You pull hair from your head, eyelashes, or eyebrows but are pretty easily able to hide the damage	Your hair pulling causes noticeable bald spots that are hard to cover, or you have pulled out so many eyelashes or brows that it's obvious that they're gone	You have to wear a wig, hat, fake eyelashes or brows, or other covering to hide the damage you've done
You spend more time than you'd like to doing the behavior, but no more than one hour per day	You spend one to two hours a day doing the behavior	You spend more than two hours a day doing the behavior
You feel a little frustrated with yourself for doing the behavior or upset with your parents for making a big deal about it	You feel really upset with yourself and a lot of embarrassment and worry about what others will think of the damage your behavior has caused	You are devastated, ashamed, and depressed about the effects of your behavior
You occasionally avoid wearing something you'd like to wear or wearing your hair a certain way, or you have to spend time applying makeup to cover the damage	You often avoid wearing certain clothing or hairstyles, avoid going places or doing things you like to do, and spend a lot of time covering up the damage	You have become isolated and rarely do things you used to enjoy due to the damage your behavior has caused

MYTH OR TRUTH?

Now it's time to test your knowledge about BFRBs by guessing whether each statement is a myth or a truth. Write an M for myth or T for truth next to each statement, and then flip to the next page for the answers.

1. BFRBs are a type of self-harm. . . . . . .
2. BFRBs are the same as a bad habit. . . . . . .
3. BFRBs tend to run in families, so if you have a BFRB, it's likely that one of your family members also has one. . . . . . .
4. People with BFRBs always know when they're doing the behavior. . . . . . .
5. If the BFRB sufferer really wanted to stop, they could. They must not be trying hard enough. . . . . . .
6. Getting rewards for the number of days you go without doing the behavior will usually help you stop doing the behavior. . . . . . .
7. Once you start doing a BFRB, you will never be able to gain control of the behavior. . . . . . .
8. There is no cure for BFRBs. . . . . . .

ANSWERS TO MYTH OR TRUTH?

1. BFRBs are a type of self-harm.

Myth: While BFRBs cause harm to the body, they are not the same as self-harming behaviors. Self-harm refers to intentionally causing physical harm or pain to distract from the emotional pain that one is feeling. People with BFRBs do not want to harm their skin or cause bald spots and usually find these behaviors self-soothing instead of painful.

2. BFRBs are the same as a bad habit.

Myth: While BFRBs are habit forming, they are much more than a bad habit. They are a psychological disorder and are a lot harder to stop than a habit. Many consider them more like an addiction, and they often require treatment in order to stop.

3. BFRBs tend to run in families, so if you have a BFRB, it's likely that one of your family members also has one.

Truth: There is a genetic component of BFRBs, meaning that it can be passed down from parents to children, but not everyone in the family will get the disorder. If you don't know of anyone in your family with a BFRB, it's likely that they have kept it hidden, and they may not even be aware that what they're doing is a BFRB. I would suggest you ask around and talk to your family members about this. You might learn a little from them and they might also learn from you and what you are reading in this book!

4. People with BFRBs always know when they're doing the behavior.

Myth: Sometimes people are aware that they are doing the behavior, and they may be looking in the mirror or directly at their skin while they're picking. We call this focused picking (or pulling, biting, chewing, etc.). Other times people are completely unaware that they're doing the behavior. This could look like pulling your hair while you're on your phone or computer, or picking your skin while in class or driving in a car. We call this automatic pulling (or picking, biting, chewing, etc.). Most people do some of both (focused and automatic), but some do just one or the other.

5. If the BFRB sufferer really wanted to stop, they could. They must not be trying hard enough.

Myth: Most people with BFRBs really want to stop but are unable to. They often try very hard, using lots of different methods. They may be able to distract themselves from doing it at times but will usually go back to doing it again. If you are one of these people, it's okay! You aren't alone! These behaviors are very difficult to stop, and they usually require professional guidance (like you're getting in this workbook) in order to find ways to consistently manage them.

6. Getting rewards for the number of days you go without doing the behavior will usually help you stop doing the behavior.

Myth: This may work for a short period of time, but eventually, you will go back to doing the behavior and then feel like a failure. It is much better to reward yourself (or have your parents reward you) **for using strategies to work towards managing the behavior** vs getting rewards for stopping the behavior. Since you don't have complete control over the behavior, it's not fair to reward you for stopping. **You will have much more long-term success by focusing on the strategies you use rather than the outcome**. So you could earn a Starbucks drink or a special outing each time you complete a chapter of this workbook. Talk to your parents and see if they're willing to help you reach these goals. If they're not, that's okay. You can still find a way to reward yourself, even if you don't have any money. Many of the adults I work with reward themselves with something like watching a favorite TV show or movie whenever they reach a goal. We'll talk more about how to create a successful reward system in Chapter 6.

7. Once you start doing a BFRB, you will never be able to gain control of the behavior.

Myth: This is a common misconception about BFRBs, but it is not true. While it is very hard to completely stop the behavior, by using the tools in this book, most people are able to gain some control of the behavior so it doesn't have as much of a negative impact on their life.

8. There is no cure for BFRBs.

Truth: There is not a cure for BFRBs, meaning that you may continue to feel urges at times and will probably never completely stop doing the behavior. However, before you give up, keep reading. It will be worth your time! While you may struggle sometimes with your BFRB throughout your life, if you consistently use the strategies taught in this book, you will be able to resist the urges most of the time and do the behavior a lot less than you're currently doing it. Doesn't that sound good?

This might look like feeling the urge to pull a hair once or twice a week and actually pulling out a few hairs every few weeks. It could also look like feeling the urge to pick your skin every few days, but when you pick you stop after one minute before any real damage is done. In order to get better, you will have to accept that it is unlikely that you will be 100% pick- or pull-free. However, you will likely feel 100 times better than you currently feel about the picking or pulling, and the damage done by the behavior will be so minimal that it will be easy to hide and won't stop you from doing the things you love anymore. There also are some people who do completely stop the behaviors or stop for several years at a time.

WHAT IS MY BFRB LIKE FOR ME?

Now that you've learned more about BFRBs in general, it's time to take a look at your particular BFRB. Answer the following questions as honestly as you can, and try not to worry about how your answers sound. This is for you and only you, so just write down whatever comes to mind.

What are the specific BFRBs that you do? If you pick your skin, where on your body do you pick? If you pull your hair, where on your body do you pull from?

....

....

How often are you doing these behaviors? For instance, do you do them every day? If so, how many times a day do you think you're doing them? If not, how many times a week are you doing them? We don't need an exact number, just your best guess.

....

....

Are you usually aware of when you're doing the behavior or are you doing it mindlessly while doing another activity like watching something on your phone or doing homework?

....

....

How do you usually feel about yourself when you do these behaviors? Many teens report feeling angry, sad, embarrassed, frustrated, or ashamed, but there are no right or wrong feelings. Whatever you feel is okay and normal.

....

....

Do you want to stop these behaviors or do them less often? If so, why? If not, why not? It's common to have mixed feelings about wanting to stop. Many teens and young adults want to stop the damage that is done when they pick or pull but also don't want to stop because it feels good or is a way to relieve stress.

....

....

GET CREATIVE

People who struggle with BFRBs often struggle with putting their feelings into words. Use the next page to express how you feel about your BFRB or what your BFRB feels like for you using your creativity. This could look like drawing, painting, making a collage of pictures from magazines or that you find online and print, or writing a poem or song about your BFRB. There is no right or wrong way to do this—just try to let go of your judgment of yourself and let your imagination and creativity take over.

I recognize that this isn't easy work, but you are making progress! Good job! You've now completed the first chapter of this book. It probably took a lot of courage and mental strength to get yourself to even pick this book up. Even if you didn't complete everything in this chapter, just by putting some effort into this, you are moving in the right direction. You now hopefully know more about BFRBs in general, and your BFRB in particular, which is the first step in tackling them.

Reminders

- ✓ Going through this book takes patience, focus, and dedication, so finding little ways to reward yourself along the way will help you to keep going. So, go buy yourself your favorite Starbucks drink or watch a show you've been waiting to watch for completing the first chapter.
- ✓ When you feel ready to move on, pick this workbook back up and keep going. Or if you're feeling like you can do a little more now, move on to the next chapter to take a little quiz to see how severe your BFRB is.
- ✓ Then we will examine how you want your life to look, which will help you find the motivation to keep going when this gets tough.
- ✓ Thinking about something that makes you feel bad about yourself isn't easy, and you may want to hide this book and just keep doing the behavior.
- ✓ It is completely normal to feel that way, **and** at the same time, you likely have some reasons for wanting to stop doing the behaviors.
- ✓ This workbook will work for you if you stick with it. The only people who won't find success with this approach are those who give up. So plan to spend a little time with this book each week, and I promise you, you won't regret it.

- CHAPTER 2 -

Do I Have a BFRB?

NOTHING TO SEE HERE

My skin, covered in red polka dots of sores head-to-toe, bleeding at random, and layered in scars, often attracted questions. But, growing up, my nickname was Yapper, and I had an answer for everything.

I'd lie about having a hard time with bug bites or allergies, or say it was chicken pox (again?). I'd even make up long stories about eccentric accidents, reasoning away the random marks on my body. It got complicated to keep them straight.

At a time I was supposed to be getting to know myself, everything about my BFRB made me feel like I was getting further and further away from who I really was.

It was confusing. And lonely.

My skin picking caused abscesses and cellulitis, frequent infections in need of oral and IV medications, extreme sleep loss, finger ligament damage, scar tissue damage, and severe carpal tunnel leading to double hand surgery. Plus, I almost lost my leg to MRSA in an area I had picked. I felt at war with my body (mind and soul).

Shame and anguish allied as constant companions. I was notorious for canceling plans, isolating, and wallowing away from family and friends. I wanted to disappear.

And alone is where I picked most.

It was an insufferable cycle. From when I woke up to when I went to sleep (even during sleep itself!), my skin picking disorder ruled my life. And then, it'd be morning again.

But understanding what I have allows me to get to know it, which makes space for me to change it. You can't change what you don't know.

Lauren McKeaney

The following is a questionnaire to help determine if you have a BFRB, and if so, how severe it is. It is called the Generic Body-Focused Repetitive Behavior Scale 8 (GBS-8).[1]

The following questions are about your BFRBs. For each item, choose the one answer that best describes the past week. If you have been having ups and downs, try to estimate an average for the past week. Please be sure to read all answers before making your choice.

1. **Frequency of the urge**: How often do you feel the urge to pick your skin, pull your hair, bite your nails, etc.?

   - ☐ 0 No urges.
   - ☐ 1 Mild: I occasionally (less than one hour per day) feel the urge to pick my skin, pull my hair, bite my nails, etc.
   - ☐ 2 Moderate: I often (one to three hours per day) feel the urge to pick my skin, pull my hair, bite my nails, etc.
   - ☐ 3 Severe: I very often (more than three and up to eight hours per day) feel the urge to pick my skin, pull my hair, bite my nails, etc.
   - ☐ 4 Extreme: I constantly or almost always feel the urge to pick my skin, pull my hair, bite my nails, etc.

2. **Intensity of the urge**: How intense or strong are the urges to pick your skin, pull your hair, bite your nails, etc.?

   - ☐ 0 Minimal or none.
   - ☐ 1 Mild.
   - ☐ 2 Moderate.
   - ☐ 3 Severe.
   - ☐ 4 Extreme.

3. **Frequency of performing BFRBs**: How much time per day do you spend picking your skin, pulling your hair, biting your nails, etc.?

   - ☐ 0 None.
   - ☐ 1 Mild: I only occasionally (less than one hour per day) pick my skin, pull my hair, bite my nails, etc.

1 Moritz, S., Gallinat, C., Weidinger, S., Bruhns, A., *et al.* (2022). 'The Generic BFRB Scale-8 (GBS-8): A transdiagnostic scale to measure the severity of body-focused repetitive behaviours.' *Behavioural and Cognitive Psychotherapy* 50, 6, 620–628.

- ☐ 2 Moderate: I frequently (one to three hours per day) pick my skin, pull my hair, bite my nails, etc.
- ☐ 3 Severe: I very frequently (more than three and up to eight hours per day) pick my skin, pull my hair, bite my nails, etc.
- ☐ 4 Extreme: I nearly constantly (more than eight hours per day) pick my skin, pull my hair, bite my nails, etc.

4. **Ability to control the urge to perform a BFRB**: How much control do you have over your skin picking, hair pulling, nail biting, etc.? To what degree can you stop yourself?

    - ☐ 0 Complete control: I am always able to stop myself from skin picking, hair pulling, nail biting, etc.
    - ☐ 1 Good control: I am usually able to stop myself from skin picking, hair pulling, nail biting, etc.
    - ☐ 2 Some control: I am sometimes able to stop myself from skin picking, hair pulling, nail biting, etc.
    - ☐ 3 Little control: I am rarely able to stop myself from skin picking, hair pulling, nail biting, etc.
    - ☐ 4 No control: I am never or almost never able to stop myself from skin picking, hair pulling, nail biting, etc.

5. **Suffering**: How much emotional distress (anxiety/worry, frustration, depression, hopelessness, or feelings of low self-esteem) do you experience from your skin picking, hair pulling, nail biting, etc.?

    - ☐ 0 None: I experience no emotional distress from my skin picking, hair pulling, nail biting, etc.
    - ☐ 1 Mild: I experience only slight emotional distress from my skin picking, hair pulling, nail biting, etc. I occasionally feel emotional distress because of it, but only to a small degree.
    - ☐ 2 Moderate: I experience a fair amount of emotional distress from my skin picking, hair pulling, nail biting, etc. I often feel emotional distress because of it.
    - ☐ 3 Severe: I experience a large amount of emotional distress from my skin picking, hair pulling, nail biting, etc. I almost always feel emotional distress because of it.
    - ☐ 4 Extreme: I experience constant emotional distress from my skin picking, hair pulling, nail biting, etc. and have no hope of this changing.

6. **Impairment**: How much does your skin picking, hair pulling, nail biting, etc. interfere with your social life or your work (or your overall functioning)? (If you are currently not working, estimate how much your performance would be affected if you were employed.)

   ☐ 0 None.
   ☐ 1 Mild: I experience slight impairment of my social or occupational activities but my overall performance is not impaired.
   ☐ 2 Moderate: I experience definite impairment of my social or occupational performance, but it is still manageable.
   ☐ 3 Severe: I experience substantial impairment of my social or occupational performance.
   ☐ 4 Extreme: I experience incapacitating impairment of my social or occupational performance.

7. **Avoidance**: Have you been avoiding doing anything, going anywhere, or being with anyone because of your skin picking, hair pulling, nail biting, etc.? If you answered "yes," then how strongly do you avoid such activities?

   ☐ 0 None (no avoidance).
   ☐ 1 Mild: I occasionally avoid social or work settings because of my skin picking, hair pulling, nail biting, etc.
   ☐ 2 Moderate: I frequently avoid social or work settings because of my skin picking, hair pulling, nail biting, etc.
   ☐ 3 Severe: I very frequently avoid social or work settings because of my skin picking, hair pulling, nail biting, etc.
   ☐ 4 Extreme: I avoid all social and work settings because of my skin picking, hair pulling, nail biting, etc.

8. **Current damage**: How much damage do you currently have because of your skin picking, hair pulling, nail biting, etc.? Only consider the damage produced by the behavior.

   ☐ 0 None (no damage).
   ☐ 1 Mild: I have slight damage in the form of small scabs, sores, scrapes, bald spots, etc. The damage covers a very small area and I do not make any attempts to hide or treat the damage.
   ☐ 2 Moderate: I have noticeable scars, scabs, small open sores, or bald

patches up to one cm in diameter. I attempt to hide or treat the damage with home remedies (e.g., bandages, creams, ointments) that do not require the assistance of a physician.

- ☐ 3 Severe: I have large scars, scabs, bald patches, open sores, infected areas, or noticeably disfigured skin. I make extensive attempts to hide the damage and may require periodic treatment by a medical professional (e.g., prescription antibiotics, dermabrasion).
- ☐ 4 Extreme: I have large open wounds or craters, frequent bleeding, large scars, bald areas, etc. The damage sometimes requires extensive covering and medical intervention (e.g., plastic surgery, stitches, hospitalization).

SCORING

Add up the numbers next to each option you selected and write your total score below.

Total score = ...

There is no official score that indicates whether you have a BFRB or not, but if you marked a 2 or higher for several of the items, then you probably meet the criteria for a BFRB.

You can also calculate a couple of sub-scores for symptom severity and impairment.

Symptom severity subscale: Add items 1, 2, 4, and the average of items 3 and 5.

Item 3 . . . . + Item 5 . . . . = ... divided by 2 (to get the average of 3 and 5) = ...

Item 1 . . . . + Item 2 . . . . + Item 4 . . . . + Average of 3 and 5 . . . . = ...

Symptom severity subscale score = ...

Impairment subscale: Add items 6, 7, and 8.

Item 6 . . . . + Item 7 . . . . + Item 8 . . . . = ...

Impairment subscale score = ...

Reminders

- ✓ You are not your BFRB. It is just one part of who you are.
- ✓ If this score is very high, it means that you have been dealing with something really hard. It does not mean that you are bad or that you won't get better. Those with the highest scores have the most opportunities for improvement.
- ✓ On the other hand, if your score is really low, that doesn't mean you don't have a BFRB. There is a wide range of severity of BFRBs, and those who score low on this questionnaire often still need help and support to manage the behaviors.
- ✓ This is just your starting point. At the end of this book, you'll take the questionnaire again to see how much better you're doing. So, wherever you are now, this is not where you'll be forever.

- CHAPTER 3 -

How Is My BFRB Affecting My Life?

AND FOR HER NEXT TRICK...

From relentless school-time bullies tearing apart my confidence like I tore my skin, to bleeding through my shirt sleeve when I went to shake my new boss's hand, my BFRB seemed to affect all areas of my life.

Living with skin picking disorder, dealing with constant skin picking episodes, taking care of their aftermath, and managing the times in between consumed my time, my wallet, and my energy.

And I was depleted.

Judging my self-worth on how good or bad my skin looked became the norm, as I (incorrectly) figured the rest of the world was doing the same. The clothes I wore (no red, as I believed it accentuated my sores), school sports I played (field hockey had leg-covering shin guards and softball had pants, unlike basketball and soccer, which required shorts), and friends I had (ones who didn't ask too many questions) felt dictated by this disorder.

Was I even authoring my own life?

My smile often masked my suffering.

Plus, a sufficient amount of magician-like deflection, caked-on concealer, and peppy personality led people to believe I was fine and flourishing. But I was raw, inside and out.

Even though I longed to, it was hard to get close to people while feeling so unsure of myself. I was so afraid of letting anyone see me, and my skin, up close and personal.

Skin picking was causing massive, unpredictable damage, controlling my existence, and there were no signs of it stopping. And I had to do what I had to do to make living with this life-pervasive disorder possible.

Looking back, I can see how a lot of what I did was just me helping me survive.

And I'm grateful for and proud of the resilience I have to endure, and overcome, what I was convinced was a life sentence.

Lauren McKeaney

Let's take a moment to think about all of the ways your BFRB impacts your life. Do you think that it has an impact on your friendships, school life, family life, the way you feel about yourself?

People who struggle with BFRBs usually aren't aware of all of the ways that their BFRB affects their lives.

Here are some examples of what other teens and young adults have reported about their BFRBs' effects on their lives. Put a checkmark next to any that you can relate to as being similar to your experience, even if the behavior isn't the same.

- ☐ "I hate the way my skin looks, and I feel so angry that I can't stop doing this to myself."
- ☐ "I'm afraid to tell my friends why I don't have eyelashes. I don't want them to think I'm weird."
- ☐ "My parents get so mad at me for picking at my mosquito bites all the time. They keep telling me to stop but I just can't."
- ☐ "I have to keep my hair in a ponytail to hide my bald spots, and I wish I could wear my hair down or in other hairstyles like all my friends."
- ☐ "It takes me so long to get ready in the morning because I have to cover up all of the damage I've done."
- ☐ "I am so frustrated that I can't stop biting my lips. They look so gross but nothing I try works."
- ☐ "When I go to school or out with friends, I'm so worried that someone will notice the bald patches on my head."
- ☐ "I can't swim with my friends because the water will wash off the makeup I use to hide all of the spots I've picked."
- ☐ "I wish I could wear the cute tank tops that my friends wear, but I'd die if one of them saw the scars on my chest, back, and shoulders."
- ☐ "I get so hot in the summer wearing pants and long-sleeved shirts to cover the scabs and open wounds from my picking."
- ☐ "I don't even want to go anywhere anymore because I know if people see my missing hair they will ask what's wrong with me."

Now, take some time to write your own statements about how your BFRB affects your life in the space below.

....

....

Take a moment to check in and notice how you feel after writing about this. It can be very hard to think about all the ways your BFRB affects you. Circle all the words that describe how you feel right now:

- ★ Ashamed
- ★ Embarrassed
- ★ Angry
- ★ Sad
- ★ Alone
- ★ Frustrated
- ★ Hurt
- ★ Lonely
- ★ Depressed
- ★ Anxious
- ★ Nervous
- ★ Jealous
- ★ Scared
- ★ Worried
- ★ Hopeful
- ★ Relieved
- ★ Calm
- ★ Relaxed
- ★ Happy

Write in any other feelings that you're experiencing now:

....

....

Now let's take a closer look at the different areas of your life that may be impacted by your BFRB. It's important to fully understand all of the negative effects that your behaviors are having on your life to help you remember why you're doing this hard work on the days you feel like giving up.

Instructions

Take some time to answer the following questions honestly. There's no right or wrong answer. Just share your experience. After each section, reflect on what you wrote and consider how this awareness can help you take steps towards change.

1. **School/work**:
   - How does your BFRB affect your schoolwork and/or job? Does picking or pulling ever slow you down when you're doing homework or make you late for school or work?

   ....

   ....

- How does it affect your concentration and productivity?

....

....

2. **Social life**:
   - How does your BFRB impact your relationships with friends and family?

   ....

   ....

   - Do you feel self-conscious or avoid certain activities because of it?

   ....

   ....

3. **Emotions/mood**:
   - Color each section of the Emotions Wheel below that lists a feeling that you experience before, during, or after you do your BFRB. You can use shading to indicate how strongly or how often you feel each of these emotions—by slightly shading in the ones that you feel only slightly and completely filling in the ones that you feel more often or more intensely.

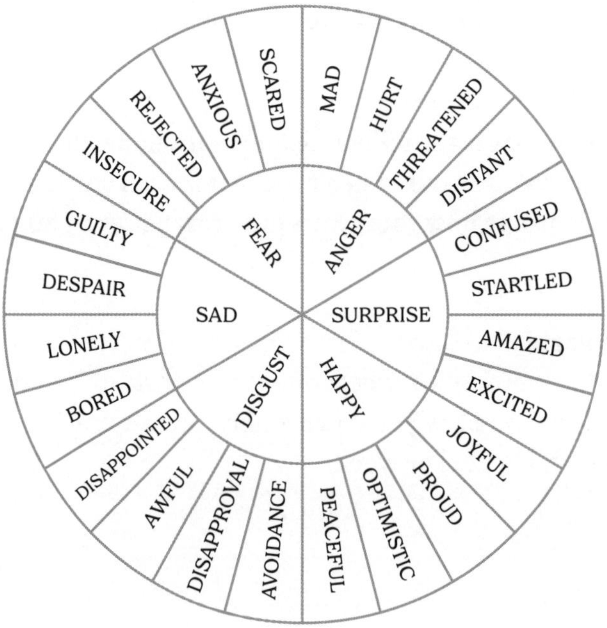

- List the emotions that you experience the most often before, during, and after engaging in your BFRB.

  ....

  ....

- How does your BFRB make you feel about yourself?

  ....

  ....

4. **Physical effects**:
   - How has your BFRB affected your physical appearance?

     ....

     ....

   - How do you feel about the way your BFRB affects your appearance?

     ....

     ....

   - Have you experienced any pain, injuries, or other health issues because of it?

     ....

     ....

Reflection

Take a few minutes to look over your answers. What stands out to you?

....

....

How does understanding the impact of your BFRB on your life help you in your journey to manage it?

....

....

Reminders

- ✓ You are not alone in this journey.
- ✓ Understanding how your BFRB affects your life is one of the most important steps towards making positive changes.
- ✓ Celebrate every small victory and remember that change takes time and effort.

PART TWO

GETTING PREPARED TO START THE PROGRAM

- CHAPTER 4 -

Setting an Intention

SEE IT TO BE IT

When I was younger, I believed I was doomed to skin pick forever.

I couldn't see how much better my life could be while working through my BFRB or how much brighter things would get once I had the right tools to help me shine.

I think what I wanted most from my BFRB was space. Room to breathe and grow and live undeniably as me. To be happy and free.

But every time I saw myself and my picked skin, I felt trapped, ugly, and less-than. And I lived from that (faulty) scale of self-worth.

One day in college, a crinkled yellow Post-it followed me home from study hall, stuck to my shoe. Inside, I stopped at my entry mirror, unfolded it, and looked at the bold smiley face I had doodled earlier. I smiled. Then I turned and saw myself in the mirror, sores and all. And stopped smiling.

But next, I almost instinctively slapped that Post-it front and center on the mirror, right at my eye level, blocking me from seeing my picked face. Staring back at that smiley face, I saw the bliss and ease I craved in my life. And seeing it felt like a chance of being it.

I had made my first vision board.

Over the next few months, when I would start my day, I'd see the smiley face Post-it before any skin irregularities that would trigger me. This allowed me to meet myself with joy and empowerment first, giving me the opportunity to begin from love. And that aligns with how I intend to live my life. And helped me take on recovery.

Lauren McKeaney

In this chapter, you will imagine what you'd like your life to be like so that you know what you're working towards. You will set an intention to help guide you through this process and motivate you to keep going when you're stuck and/ or feeling defeated.

STEP 1: IMAGINING MY FUTURE SELF AFTER RECOVERING FROM A BFRB

Instructions

Find a quiet place where you can think deeply and write freely. Take your time with each section, and let your imagination guide you as you picture your future self.

Take a few minutes to settle into the exercise by closing your eyes and taking some slow, deep breaths. Put one or both hands on your stomach and see if you can feel your belly (diaphragm) fill up like a balloon as you slowly breathe in. Pause and then slowly let your breath flow back out as you feel your belly deflate. Take three or four breaths like this, noticing each in breath and each out breath.

1. **Visualizing my future**:
   - Close your eyes and imagine yourself in the future, successfully managing your BFRB.
     - ▹ How do you look? Describe your appearance, including how your hair, skin, or nails have changed, and/or draw in the space below to show the changes in your appearance.

       ....

       ....

     - ▹ Where are you in this future scenario? Are you at school, work, home, or somewhere special?

       ....

       ....

     - ▹ Who is with you, if anyone? How do they see and interact with you?

       ....

       ....

2. **My daily life as my future self**:
   - **Describe a typical day in your life after recovering from your BFRB.**
     - ▹ How do you start your day? What are your morning routines?

       ....

       ....

     - ▹ What activities do you do throughout the day?

       ....

       ....

     - ▹ What hobbies or interests have you developed?

       ....

       ....

   - **How do you feel throughout the day?**
     - ▹ What emotions are most common for you now?

       ....

       ....

     - ▹ How do you manage challenges or setbacks?

       ....

       ....

3. **My relationships**:
   - **How have your relationships with others changed?**
     - ▹ How do you interact with your friends, family, or romantic partner?

       ....

       ....

     - ▹ How do you feel about social situations now?

       ....

       ....

- **What do others say about the changes they've seen in you?**
  - Imagine a conversation with a close friend or family member about your journey. What do they notice about the "new" you?

    ....

    ....

4. **My self-perception**:
   - **How do you see yourself now?**

     ....

     ....

     - What are the three words that best describe your future self?

       ....

       ....

     - How has your confidence changed?

       ....

       ....

   - **What is your self-talk like?**
     - How do you talk to yourself when you face challenges?

       ....

       ....

     - What positive affirmations or reminders do you give yourself?

       ....

       ....

Reflection

Take a few moments to read what you've written. How does imagining your future self make you feel?

....

....

....

What part of this vision excites you the most?

....

....

How can you keep this vision in mind as you continue working towards recovery?

....

....

STEP 2: CREATING A VISION BOARD FOR MY FUTURE SELF

Let's get creative! A vision board is a powerful tool that helps you visualize your goals and dreams. In this activity, you'll create a vision board that represents your future self after overcoming your BFRB. This will serve as a daily reminder of the life you're working towards.

Materials Needed

- A poster board or large piece of paper
- Magazines, newspapers, or printed images
- Scissors
- Glue or tape
- Markers, pens, or colored pencils
- Optional: Stickers, washi tape, or other decorative items

Instructions

1. **Set your intention**:
    - **Reflect on your future self**: Take a few minutes to think about what your life will look like once you've managed your BFRB. Reread your answers from the previous exercise and add any new details or ideas that you have.
    - **Choose a focus**: Decide on a central theme for your vision board. It could be "Confidence," "Peace," "Freedom from BFRBs," or any word or phrase that resonates with your vision.

2. **Gather images and words**:
   - **Search for inspiration**: Flip through magazines, newspapers, or online resources to find images and words that reflect your vision of the future. Look for pictures that make you feel positive and inspired, as well as words or phrases that capture the essence of your future self.
   - **Cut and collect**: Carefully cut out these images and words. You can also print out images from the internet or draw your own if you can't find exactly what you're looking for.

3. **Arrange and create your vision board**:
   - **Lay out your vision**: Before you start gluing, arrange the images and words on your poster board. Think about how you want to organize them. You might group them by theme (e.g., relationships, self-care, goals) or create a collage that blends everything together.
   - **Add your focus word or phrase**: Place your central theme or focus word prominently on your vision board. This should be something you see right away when you look at it.
   - **Glue everything in place**: Once you're happy with the arrangement, start gluing the images and words onto the board. Feel free to overlap images or leave some space—this is your personal creation.

4. **Personalize your vision board**:
   - **Add finishing touches**: Use markers, pens, or colored pencils to add any personal touches. You might write affirmations, doodle, or add quotes that motivate you. Stickers, washi tape, or other decorations can make your board even more unique.
   - **Make it yours**: This is your vision board, so it should reflect your personal style and goals. Don't worry about making it perfect—what matters is that it inspires you.

5. **Display your vision board**:
   - **Choose a special spot**: Place your vision board somewhere you'll see it every day, like your bedroom wall, the inside of your locker, on your bathroom mirror, or above your desk. The more you see it, the more it will remind you of the future you're working towards.
   - **Reflect and revise**: Take a moment each day to look at your vision board and think about the steps you're taking towards becoming your future self. As you grow and change, you might want to add new images or adjust your board to reflect your evolving goals.

Reflection

After completing your vision board, write a few sentences about how it makes you feel. How does seeing your future self on the board motivate you?

....

....

....

....

STEP 3: SETTING MY INTENTION

As you reflect on all of the ways that your BFRB currently affects your life (review Chapter 3 if it's been a minute) and consider this vision you've created for your future self, you have a few questions to seriously consider.

1. Do you want to work towards making this vision a reality?

☐ Yes
☐ No

If you answered "yes," continue to the next question.

If you answered "no," then you should put this book away and pull it back out if you change your mind.

2. Do you have the time and energy to commit to working about 10–20 minutes per day on these exercises over the next 10 weeks in order to become this future self you've envisioned (or at least pretty close to it)?

☐ Yes
☐ No

If you answered "yes," continue to the next question.

If you answered "no," put this book down until you do have the time and energy to commit to this. Remember, there is never a perfect time, but if now really is not a good time to try to start this, then it's better to wait a bit until you are ready.

3. Are you willing to make the commitment to work as hard as you can over the next 10 weeks to make this vision a reality for you?

   ☐ Yes
   ☐ No

   If you answered "yes," move on to setting your intention.

   If you answered "no," take a moment to think about what is holding you back. Is it something that you can talk through with someone to help resolve it? Are your parents forcing you to do this? If so, can you talk to them about it or seek the help of a professional (school counselor, doctor, therapist, etc.) or a trusted adult (teacher, family member, friend, etc.)? In order to make progress in this program, you need to acknowledge that your BFRB is a problem and want to make some changes. You don't need to completely stop the behavior, but you will need to put considerable time and effort into this program in order for it to work. If you're not ready to at least give it a try, then it's probably not the right time for you to do this.

Setting My Intention for BFRB Recovery

State your commitment to this workbook in one sentence. For example, "I will work as hard as I can over the next 10 weeks to complete every activity in this workbook so that I can live the life I want to live without my BFRB holding me back."

My Intention

....

....

....

....

....

....

....

....

Finding a Spot for My Intention

Choose a place or two where you will put your intention so that you will be reminded of it over the next 10 weeks. Here are some ideas. Check off the ones that you will use.

- ☐ Write your intention on an index card or Post-it note and place it in a spot that you will see often.
- ☐ Type your intention, print it, and cut out the sentence. Glue or tape it onto your vision board.
- ☐ Write your intention in your planner or on your calendar.
- ☐ Tell someone what your intention is to help hold yourself accountable.
- ☐ Take a picture of yourself holding your intention, print it, and put it up on your mirror to remind you of what you're working towards.
- ☐ Other: Write your own ideas below of other ways to keep your intention in mind.

....

....

Reminders

- ✓ You have the power to make changes in your life in order to become the person you want to become.
- ✓ Your BFRB does not have to hold you back from doing anything you want to do.
- ✓ Keeping a vision in mind of how you'd like your life to look is a powerful step towards recovery from your BFRB.
- ✓ Over time, it's normal for your motivation to fade, so your vision board and your intention statement will be very important tools to help get you back on track when you start to lose hope.

- CHAPTER 5 -

Involving Parents or Other Loved Ones (or Getting Them to Back Off)

HELP ME HELP YOU

Even though my loved ones meant well, their efforts along my skin picking journey weren't always helpful. They constantly pleaded for me to "Stop picking!" and I agreed! That's what I wanted to do too!

But how?!

I felt ashamed by the ripped, crusted, discolored appearance of my skin, yes. But more so, how I couldn't do what my family suggested was so simple, stop skin picking. I knew they wanted to help. But I wasn't sure how to help them help me.

Over time, I learned that understanding my boundaries, and recognizing where people are with respecting them, was a key part of my recovery. It allowed me to better navigate how I involve others in my healing process.

Consider creating a sharing script to guide your sharing once you decide who is on your support team. This preparation will permit you to speak freely while saying what you need to say, lessening getting overwhelmed and tongue-tied in the moment. (I've been there.)

Remember that not everyone needs to know everything. You can share as much or as little as you want to. And it's helpful to let people know if you're looking for input or listening.

Work with your loved ones to determine their learning languages. Based on how they consume information, I might send my mom a BFRB article to read and send my sister a skin picking meme on social media from the Picking Me Foundation @pickingmefdn. Both approaches meet them where they are and help them engage with me in a way that feels supportive and real.

Lauren McKeaney

PART 1: SHOULD I TELL ANYONE?

Deciding whether or not to involve your parents, friends, or other loved ones can be really tough. There are lots of ways it can help you, but there's also a risk of getting hurt in some situations. Here are some questions to help you figure out what's best for you in each of your important relationships.

My Inner Circle

Start by making a list of the people who are closest to you.

1. ....

2. ....

3. ....

4. ....

5. ....

Now go back and write three words that best describe your relationship with each person you listed above, and then two feelings that you most often feel when you're with this person. Don't overthink which words or feelings to choose—just write down what first comes to mind for each person.

My Support System

Now list five people who you consider to be your biggest supporters. This could include the same people who are in your inner circle, or it may not. Just write the names of the first five people who come to mind when you think of your support system.

1. ....

2. ....

3. ....

4. ....

5. ....

Next to each of these names, write the first two words that come to mind when you think about how they support you and two feelings that you feel when you think of them.

Who Should I Tell?

Keeping in mind the work you did above, make a list of three people you are considering telling about your BFRB. You can always add more later, so just pick the three who you're feeling most curious about whether or not to tell them. These three people could be on one, both, or neither of the lists above. Sometimes the people you want to tell may surprise you!

1. ....
2. ....
3. ....

Now, next to each name, write a fear that comes to mind when you think of telling this person, and then write two feelings that you think you might feel after telling them.

Questions to Determine Whether to Tell a Loved One

These first exercises have hopefully helped you to start identifying who you might tell and what your thoughts and feelings about telling them might be. Now, you'll go more in depth with each of the people you're considering telling.

Person 1's name: ....

How could telling this person potentially help me? Circle all that apply:

They can hand me a fidget when I need one.

They can help me notice when I'm doing it.

They can help me reward myself when I use a strategy.

They can support me when I'm feeling frustrated or sad.

It will help us get closer.

They can hold my hand.

Add your own ideas about how telling them could help you:

....

....

....

How could not telling them hurt me?

I won't be able to get support from them about this.

I'd have to keep hiding it, which is hard.

Keeping this secret puts some distance between us.

When I'm upset with myself for doing the behavior, I can't talk to them about it.

They can't be proud of me when I make progress.

How else could not telling them make my life harder?

....

....

....

....

How supportive is this person in my life?

5 Extremely supportive
4 Very supportive
3 Pretty supportive
2 Somewhat supportive
1 A little supportive
0 Not supportive

How likely is it that they will be supportive about this?

5 Extremely likely
4 Very likely
3 Pretty likely
2 Somewhat likely
1 A little likely
0 Not likely

How much do I trust this person?

5 100% without a doubt
4 Very much
3 Pretty much
2 Somewhat
1 A little bit
0 0% Not at all

Does this person often do things that hurt me or others?

- ☐ Yes, very often
- ☐ Somewhat often
- ☐ No, not very often

Do the potential benefits outweigh the potential risks?

- ☐ Yes
- ☐ No

Considering all of the above, will you tell this person?

- ☐ Yes
- ☐ No

If you answered "yes," move on to the next set of questions to determine how to tell them.

If you answered "no," is there anything that would make it more likely that you'd tell them in the future?

....

....

Are there any questions you could ask them or discussions you could have that would make you feel more comfortable telling them?

....

....

Person 2's name: ....

How could telling this person potentially help me? Circle all that apply:

They can hand me a fidget when I need one.

They can help me notice when I'm doing it.

They can help me reward myself when I use a strategy.

They can support me when I'm feeling frustrated or sad.

It will help us get closer.

They can hold my hand.

Add your own ideas about how telling them could help you:

....

....

How could not telling them hurt me?

I won't be able to get support from them about this.

I'd have to keep hiding it, which is hard.

Keeping this secret puts some distance between us.

When I'm upset with myself for doing the behavior, I can't talk to them about it.

They can't be proud of me when I make progress.

How else could not telling them make my life harder?

....

How supportive is this person in my life?

5 Extremely supportive
4 Very supportive
3 Pretty supportive
2 Somewhat supportive
1 A little supportive
0 Not supportive

How likely is it that they will be supportive about this?

5 Extremely likely
4 Very likely
3 Pretty likely
2 Somewhat likely
1 A little likely
0 Not likely

How much do I trust this person?

5 100% without a doubt
4 Very much
3 Pretty much
2 Somewhat
1 A little bit
0 0% Not at all

Does this person often do things that hurt me or others?

- ☐ Yes, very often
- ☐ Somewhat often
- ☐ No, not very often

Do the potential benefits outweigh the potential risks?

- ☐ Yes
- ☐ No

Considering all of the above, will you tell this person?

- ☐ Yes
- ☐ No

If you answered "yes," move on to the next set of questions to determine how to tell them.

If you answered "no," is there anything that would make it more likely that you'd tell them in the future?

....

....

Are there any questions you could ask them or discussions you could have that would make you feel more comfortable telling them?

....

....

Person 3's name: ....

How could telling this person potentially help me? Circle all that apply:

They can hand me a fidget when I need one.

They can help me notice when I'm doing it.

They can help me reward myself when I use a strategy.

They can support me when I'm feeling frustrated or sad.

It will help us get closer.

They can hold my hand.

Add your own ideas about how telling them could help you:

....

....

How could not telling them hurt me?

I won't be able to get support from them about this.

I'd have to keep hiding it, which is hard.

Keeping this secret puts some distance between us.

When I'm upset with myself for doing the behavior, I can't talk to them about it.

They can't be proud of me when I make progress.

How else could not telling them make my life harder?

....

How supportive is this person in my life?

5 Extremely supportive
4 Very supportive
3 Pretty supportive
2 Somewhat supportive
1 A little supportive
0 Not supportive

How likely is it that they will be supportive about this?

5 Extremely likely
4 Very likely
3 Pretty likely
2 Somewhat likely
1 A little likely
0 Not likely

How much do I trust this person?

5 100% without a doubt
4 Very much
3 Pretty much
2 Somewhat
1 A little bit
0 0% Not at all

Does this person often do things that hurt me or others?

- ☐ Yes, very often
- ☐ Somewhat often
- ☐ No, not very often

Do the potential benefits outweigh the potential risks?

- ☐ Yes
- ☐ No

Considering all of the above, will you tell this person?

- ☐ Yes
- ☐ No

If you answered "yes," move on to the next set of questions to determine how to tell them.

If you answered "no," is there anything that would make it more likely that you'd tell them in the future?

....

....

Are there any questions you could ask them or discussions you could have that would make you feel more comfortable telling them?

....

....

PART 2: HOW DO I TELL THEM?

Now that you've decided to tell someone, how on earth are you going to do it? To prepare yourself to share this very personal information, there are a few more things to consider.

Why do you want to tell this person about your BFRB? (Check all that apply)

- ☐ To feel less alone

- ☐ To help them understand what I'm going through
- ☐ To get support
- ☐ To explain certain behaviors
- ☐ To be honest
- ☐ Something else: ....

How might they react? Think about how this person might respond to hearing about your BFRB. What emotions might they experience?

- ☐ Surprised
- ☐ Confused
- ☐ Concerned
- ☐ Supportive
- ☐ Curious
- ☐ Worried
- ☐ Something else: ....

Why might they feel this way?

....

....

What might they need to know? What information can you share to help them understand your BFRB better? (E.g., what it is, why it happens, that it's not something you can easily control, etc.)

....

....

Write down what you want to say. It can be helpful to write down your thoughts before the conversation. Here's a starting point:

> "There's something important I want to share with you about myself."
>
> "I have something called a Body-Focused Repetitive Behavior, which means I do things like .... when I'm feeling stressed or overwhelmed."

Now, write your specific message:

....

....

....

....

Decide whether to tell them in person, over video chat, on the phone, or over text or email. There is no right or wrong way to tell them. How would you feel most comfortable telling them?

....

Choose the right time and place. Think about when and where you want to have this conversation or send this email. Choose a time when you're calm, and in a private, comfortable place where you won't be interrupted.

Best time: ....

Best place: ....

Prepare for their possible reactions. Imagine how the conversation might go. What are some ways the person might react? How can you respond if they...

...ask questions?

....

....

...don't understand right away?

....

....

...react negatively or dismissively?

....

....

...want to help?

....

....

Having this conversation might make you feel nervous, and that is okay and totally normal! What can you do to stay calm during the conversation? (E.g., take deep breaths, remind yourself you're doing something brave, etc.)

After the conversation, reflect on how it went:

How did you feel after sharing?

....

....

What went well?

....

....

What could have gone better?

....

....

What support do you need now?

....

....

After sharing about your BFRB, what kind of support do you need from the person you told or from others in your life? (E.g., ongoing conversations, emotional support, or just knowing they understand.)

....

....

Remember, sharing something as personal as this takes a lot of courage. No matter how the conversation went, be proud of yourself for taking this step.

PART 3: HOW DO I DEAL WITH THE PEOPLE (USUALLY PARENTS) WHO ARE MAKING MY BFRB WORSE?

It is no surprise to any of us that there are and will be people in your life who, when they find out about your BFRB, instead of being helpful, actually make it worse. First, let's identify what they're doing to make it worse.

Think of three people who sometimes (or often) make your BFRB worse.

1. ....

2. ....

3. ....

How do each of these people impact your BFRB? Next to each person's name, write down how they impact your BFRB. Do they unintentionally increase your stress or anxiety? Do they say or do things that make you feel worse? Or do they sometimes help but also make things harder in certain ways?

- **Person 1:**
    - Impact: ....
    - Example: ....
- **Person 2:**
    - Impact: ....
    - Example: ....
- **Person 3:**
    - Impact: ....
    - Example: ....

What are the specific things that they do that make your BFRB worse? Check all that apply, and write your own if needed:

- ☐ Criticizing or judging me.
- ☐ Pointing out my BFRB in front of others.
- ☐ Pressuring me to stop.
- ☐ Ignoring my feelings.
- ☐ Making jokes about it.
- ☐ Creating stressful situations.
- ☐ Something else: ....

Describe a situation. Choose one recent situation where someone's actions or words made your BFRB worse. Describe what happened and how it affected you:

....

....

....

....

Analyzing Patterns

Are there patterns? Look back at what you've written. Do you notice any patterns? For example, does your BFRB get worse around certain people, in specific situations, or when certain topics come up?

....

....

How do these patterns affect your life? How does the way others affect your BFRB impact your daily life? Does it make you more anxious, less confident, or more isolated?

....

....

Setting Boundaries and Communicating Needs

What do you need from others? Think about how others could be more supportive or less triggering for your BFRB. Write down what you need from them to help you manage your behavior in a healthier way:

....

....

....

....

How can you communicate this? Consider how you might express these needs to the people in your life. What could you say to help them understand without making them feel defensive?

Here's a starting point:

- "I know you care about me, and I need to talk to you about something that's been affecting me..."
- "When you ...., it makes my BFRB worse. It would help if you could .... instead."

Now, write down what you might say:

....

....

Setting Healthy Boundaries

Think about how you can set boundaries with the people who make your BFRB worse, even if they don't mean to. What are some boundaries you could set to protect your well-being?

- Let the person know that you will have to spend less time with them if they continue to do or say things that make your BFRB worse. Make sure to be clear and kind in how you say this so that they can hear the message without getting defensive. For instance, "I feel sad and frustrated when you keep bringing up my BFRB so I will leave the room when you bring it up."

- Point it out in the moment when someone says something hurtful, and then walk away or get some space from them. For example, "I already know that I'm pulling, and when you point it out to me, I feel worse, which makes me pull more. I'm going to spend some time away from you now."

- Limit the amount of time you spend with the people who make your BFRB worse.

- If necessary and possible, end the relationship with the person who consistently makes you feel worse if you've tried to communicate all of the above to them and they are still not respecting your wishes. (This applies more to friendships and other relationships, as you cannot end the relationship with a family member but rather just limit the time you spend with them.)
- Write the person a letter explaining how what they're doing is hurting you and how they can do better.

Other boundaries:

....

....

What challenges might you face? We know that setting boundaries can be hard, especially with adults or other people you care about. What hurdles do you think you might face when trying to set these boundaries? How can you handle them?

....

....

Great! You are making progress! Now that you know who is in your support system, who is not, and how to best communicate with them, you can move to the next chapter to set up a plan for support and accountability as you work through this workbook.

Reminders

✓ It's important to take time to consider who you want to tell about your BFRB.

✓ Loved ones can often provide much-needed support if you let them.

✓ Make sure to tell them what is helpful and what is not.

✓ Use boundaries to protect yourself from those in your life who aren't supportive.

- CHAPTER 6 -

Creating Your Support System

TEAM MANAGEMENT

For decades I didn't have the language (or available diagnosis) to explain what I couldn't explain, which made it difficult to live, let alone let people in.

But the more I understood my BFRB, the more I was able to involve my loved ones on my journey towards managing it.

I remember this one time, my mom and I were exhausted from another cycle of me having picked, her catching me, and me denying it. She said she was going to head to the store for a minute and asked if I needed anything. I joked, "Well, Band-Aids!"

So she brought me back a box of 50 Band-Aids. And we put on the Band-Aids. All 50 of them.

There we were, doing something about it. Together. We weren't saying anything, but our actions spoke so loud. I felt supported and protected. By the Band-Aids, too.

Friends felt hard to tell. I was too embarrassed to be different (in this way).

I couldn't imagine asking a friend to be an accountability partner for helping manage my skin picking.

But I'm so glad I did.

One way I started to practice working on and rewarding my goal for my BFRB in everyday life was by asking my friend if she wanted to join me for my reward manicure. Not only did I honor myself for a goal I'd met, but I also got to spend quality time with a bestie, while productively managing my skin picking with nail care.

I felt accomplished, while bonding and having a good time. I couldn't wait to do it again.

Rewards come in all shapes and sizes, though.

One of my fav go-to rewards to this day is hitting snooze again. Do I want and look forward to doing that? Sometimes. Can I turn it into some motivation, like getting to hit snooze tomorrow if I finish another chapter in this workbook tonight? Why not!

Lauren McKeaney

Based on the people you identified in Chapter 5 who are most supportive (hooray for these people!), you'll now come up with a plan for how you will get support while working through this workbook. Before we dive into that, though, we will first describe how and why support and accountability are so helpful.

WHY ARE ACCOUNTABILITY AND SUPPORT SO IMPORTANT AND NECESSARY AS I GO THROUGH THIS WORKBOOK?

Motivation to Keep Going

In order to make changes when it comes to your BFRB, you will have to devote a lot of time and effort to the steps outlined in this workbook. Kind of like a typical school year, it's very common to start off strong in your desire to do this work; however, over time, people often lose some of this motivation and either slow down or give up. Those who have people supporting them and checking in on their progress (accountability) tend to stay motivated or regain their motivation if it starts to fade.

Someone to Lean on During the Hard Times

Some of the things that you'll be asked to do in this workbook will likely bring up thoughts and feelings that are difficult to handle. It's helpful to have someone who will check in on you and help you work through these emotions. Or, if you don't feel like talking, they can be there to sit with you while you do the work or do something fun with you to help lift your mood.

Cheerleading and Rewards (Trust Me—This Does Not Get Cheesy!)

As you do the hard work, it is also very helpful to have someone there to celebrate your successes and to remind you to reward yourself for the efforts you're putting into this. By setting up a plan for this ahead of time, you won't have to reach out and tell someone of your successes (because that can be very hard to do). Instead, they will be checking in on you and will naturally hear about your accomplishments. They can also then be a part of your reward system, such as buying you something or coming with you to do a fun thing!

WHO WILL I INCLUDE IN MY SUPPORT SYSTEM?

Based on the work you did in Chapter 5, who are the people you'd like to help support you through this workbook? List one to three people below:

1. ....
2. ....
3. ....

If you cannot think of anyone to help support you, I recommend that you find a therapist to work with as you go through this workbook. Visit www.bfrb.org and use their therapist directory to find one near you.

There are lots of different ways that your support people can check in. Here are some examples of ways someone can step up to help you when you need it and also help hold you accountable. Check any that sound like something you might like one of your support people to try.

WAYS TO PROVIDE SUPPORT

Emotional Support

- ☐ **Listen without judgment**: You will express your feelings, frustrations, and challenges, and your supporter will just listen without making any comments.
- ☐ **Validate your experience**: They will acknowledge what you're struggling with and remind you that you're not alone in dealing with it.
- ☐ **Offer encouragement**: They will consistently remind you of your progress, no matter how small, and boost your confidence to keep going.

Helping with Self-Care

- ☐ **Suggest calming or grounding techniques**: Offer to practice deep breathing, mindfulness, or other stress-relieving activities with you.
- ☐ **Remind you of self-care routines**: Encourage habits like getting enough rest, eating well, and taking breaks during the day to help reduce triggers.

Being a Positive Distraction

- ☐ **Engage in fun activities with you (of course, if you feel like it!)**: Doing activities like going for walks, playing a game, or watching a movie can help you stay distracted from your BFRB urges.
- ☐ **Help you find new hobbies or interests**: Encouraging creative or physical activities like drawing, sports, or crafts can provide healthy outlets for you.

Creating a Non-Judgmental Space

- ☐ **Avoid blaming or shaming**: Your supporter will strive to never criticize or make you feel guilty when you engage in your BFRB. Instead, they will focus on being compassionate and patient.
- ☐ **Celebrate small victories**: Your supporter can acknowledge even the smallest steps in your journey to show you that they recognize your effort and growth.

Providing Resources or Tools

- ☐ **Help you find coping tools**: Introduce fidget toys, stress balls, or mindfulness apps that may help with the urge to engage in your BFRB.
- ☐ **Educate themselves**: Your supporter will read through sections of this workbook and/or other resources to learn more about BFRBs and your specific behaviors and coping strategies.

WAYS TO PROVIDE ACCOUNTABILITY

Regular Check-Ins

- ☐ **Weekly or daily check-ins**: Ask you how you're feeling and how you've been managing your BFRB.
- ☐ **Progress updates**: Ask you about any progress you've made.

Reviewing Goals

- ☐ **Help set goals**: Your supporter could work with you to set goals each week based on the material you learn in this book.

- ☐ **Hold you accountable for those goals**: Gently remind you about the goals you set and ask how you are working towards them.

Gentle Reminders or Prompts

- ☐ **Subtle reminders**: If they notice you engaging in your BFRB, offer a gentle nudge or grab your hand gently. They could also hand you a fidget or ask if you want to get up and do something with them. You will decide exactly how and when they can remind you.
- ☐ **Set up reminders together**: Help you set alarms or reminders on your phone to remind you to use a strategy.

Helping with Your Reward System

- ☐ **Track progress and rewards**: Help you set up a reward system where you get a small reward after reaching specific milestones (more to come on this in a bit).
- ☐ **Offer positive reinforcement**: Praise you for sticking to your plan or trying new coping strategies, even if it wasn't perfect.

Practicing Together

- ☐ **Participate in coping strategies**: Practice alternative coping strategies together, like doing a meditation together or talking through some thought challenging.
- ☐ **Read through this workbook together**: Sit down together and go through a chapter, talking through the activities and your responses.

MY PLAN FOR SUPPORT AND ACCOUNTABILITY

A little heads up for you—your needs will probably change as you go through this program, and it's hard to identify ahead of time what you'll need. However, the more you can set up ahead of time, the better your chances of success. So, I recommend setting up a plan now, knowing that you can (and probably will) change it often.

Fill in the chart below with the names of people who you'd like to check in on your progress regularly. Then list how often you want them to check in and what type of check-in works best. See the example below, and then fill in your own chart.

Example

Name	Check-in frequency	Check-in method
Alex	Weekly	Text
Mom	Every other day	In person

My Check-In Plan

Name	Check-in frequency	Check-in method

Creating My Reward Plan

Rewards can be hard, but they don't have to be. They can actually be really fun and motivating. You will simply be creating a plan to earn a reward when you complete a goal. This is sometimes done with the help of parents' financial or other support, but it can also definitely be done on your own. I strongly encourage every client I see with a BFRB, including adults, to use a reward system.

Who needs rewards?

- We all need incentives to help us get and stay motivated.
- Research has shown that positive reward systems are more motivating than those based on penalties or punishments. Let's be honest—no one wants that!
- This workbook involves putting in some effort, and many teens (and adults) will stop pushing themselves to do the hard work without a reward system in place.

But I don't need one because (check all that apply):

- ☐ Rewards are for little kids.
- ☐ The reward will be my hair growth or clear skin.
- ☐ I can do this without a reward.
- ☐ I already get everything I want.
- ☐ There's no reward that will get me to stop picking or pulling.
- ☐ There's no point in creating this system, because I won't earn any rewards.
- ☐ I don't deserve to get a reward.

Despite these common objections, rewards are recommended for every person of any age. Rewards are actually commonly used by older teens and adults without them realizing that they are actually rewards. For instance, ask your parents if they would still go to work every day if they didn't get paid. Getting paid for working is a reward.

Rewards are central to the behavioral principle of positive reinforcement, which is what encourages all humans (and animals) to change their behavior. If you have a dog in your home or have a friend with a dog, try to see if you can teach them to sit or shake without a treat. Some dogs may respond if they are rewarded by you saying "good job" in an upbeat tone of voice or by the reward of you smiling and petting them. However, most dogs will learn this new behavior much more quickly with the use of a treat, because dogs are usually very motivated by tasty food (most humans are too). So, if you want to change your behavior, you will be much more successful if you choose rewards that are motivating to you.

Before you choose your rewards, we'll first choose goals to work on in order to earn rewards.

Choosing goals

As you review the work you've done in this chapter, make a list of things you need to do to set up your Support and Accountability Plan. This might include things like calling your mom and telling her that you'd like her to ask you once every three days how you're doing and texting your best friend to let her know that you'd like to meet at Starbucks every Sunday to have someone there with you as you go through each chapter of the workbook.

Things I need to do to set up my Support and Accountability Plan:

1. ....

2. ....

3. ....

4. ....

5. ....

If any of these tasks seems too hard to do quickly and easily, see if you can break them down into smaller steps.

Broken-down steps:

1. ....

2. ....

3. ....

4. ....

5. ....

6. ....

7. ....

Ideas for rewards

Here's a list of some ideas of rewards, broken down into different categories. Put a checkmark next to any that you think might motivate you and then add some more of your own at the end of each category.

Fun and leisure rewards

- ☐ Extra screen time (phone, gaming, TV)
- ☐ Movie night (at home or theater)
- ☐ Favorite snacks or desserts
- ☐ Shopping trip for clothes or accessories
- ☐ Sleepover with friends
- ☐ Tickets to a concert, sports event, or amusement park
- ☐ Special outing (bowling, mini-golf, ice skating)
- ☐ Music playlist control for a day
- ☐ Other fun and/or leisure rewards: ....

Privileges

- ☐ Later bedtime for a week
- ☐ Extra time with friends or outings
- ☐ Choice of family activity for the weekend
- ☐ Extended curfew for a night
- ☐ Freedom to redecorate or rearrange your room
- ☐ Extra car privileges (for licensed teens and adults)
- ☐ Other privileges you'd like as rewards: ....

Educational/creative rewards

- ☐ New books, art supplies, or learning tools
- ☐ Access to online classes (coding, photography, design)
- ☐ Subscription to a service (Spotify, Netflix, etc.)
- ☐ Craft or DIY project kit
- ☐ Time at a café or library for personal study
- ☐ Journaling or sketchbook materials
- ☐ Other educational and/or creative rewards: ....

Tech and gadget rewards

- ☐ New phone accessories (case, charger, headphones)
- ☐ Gift cards for apps, games, or music
- ☐ Paid downloads for a game, movie, or app upgrade
- ☐ Bluetooth speaker or smart gadget
- ☐ Other tech and/or gadget rewards: ....

Physical activities and wellness Rewards

- ☐ Membership or passes to a gym, yoga, or fitness class
- ☐ Outdoor adventure day (hiking, kayaking, biking)
- ☐ Sports equipment upgrade or clothing
- ☐ Time at a trampoline park or climbing gym
- ☐ Other physical activities and/or wellness rewards:....................

Family or social time rewards

- ☐ Family game night with your favorite games
- ☐ A special dinner where you choose the menu
- ☐ Invite friends over for a themed party
- ☐ A cooking or baking day with a parent or sibling
- ☐ Other family or social time rewards:..................................

Money-related rewards

- ☐ Cash allowance for a certain achievement
- ☐ Gift cards to your favorite stores or brands

- ☐ Savings matching for a future purchase (e.g., car, computer)
- ☐ Other money-related rewards: ....

Personal growth rewards

- ☐ Career exploration day (e.g., shadowing someone at work)
- ☐ Volunteer hours for a cause you care about
- ☐ Subscription box (books, snacks, self-care)
- ☐ Learning a new skill (private lessons in a subject of your interest)
- ☐ Journaling prompts for self-reflection and development
- ☐ Other personal growth rewards: ....

Next, it's time to make a list of your specific rewards. Start with jotting down any of the above items that you checked that you'd like to earn as rewards and then add anything else that comes to mind when you think about what you want. Break them up into small, medium, and large rewards.

Small rewards
(E.g., candy, downloading a song, taking a walk with someone, watching a show, etc.)

1. ....
2. ....
3. ....
4. ....
5. ....
6. ....
7. ....
8. ....

Medium rewards
(E.g., a Starbucks drink, manicure, new shirt, choosing where to go out to eat, etc.)

1. ....
2. ....

3. ....

4. ....

5. ....

6. ....

7. ....

8. ....

Large rewards
(E.g., pair of shoes, video game, out to eat with a friend, shopping trip, etc.)

1. ....

2. ....

3. ....

4. ....

5. ....

6. ....

7. ....

8. ....

Putting it all together

Progress is being made! The final step is deciding how many goals or tasks you have to complete in order to get a reward. Some people prefer to get a small reward daily, while others prefer to get a medium-sized reward after a week or so's worth of work or a large reward after a few weeks or months of work. This part really depends on who, if anyone, is helping with the reward plan. If you have a parent or other person who is going to pay for the rewards, then you'll have to discuss what works for them. Some teens choose to do the plan without their parents for various reasons. It's really up to you.

TIPS

- Start out easy. Choose a very doable task and give yourself a reward for completing it.
- Choose goals that you have control over, such as using a strategy or trying an exercise, rather than setting the goal for you to stop doing the behavior.
- Reward yourself even if you don't fully complete the goal. The point is that you want to encourage yourself to work on this, so as long as you're moving in the right direction, it's helpful to get a reward, especially in the beginning when you're trying to develop healthier behaviors.
- Keep track of your goals and points for completing them on a weekly chart.

My Reward Chart

Goal	Mon	Tue	Wed	Thu	Fri	Sat	Sun

How to earn rewards

- 1 point for each step of a task completed
- 3 points = small reward
- 10 points = medium reward
- 25 points = large reward

Reminders

- ✓ Most people will achieve their goals more quickly and with less pain and suffering if they have a solid support system.
- ✓ Your support needs may change over time, so just give this plan a try and then adjust as needed.
- ✓ All humans (and most animals too) need rewards in order to achieve their goals.
- ✓ You will be much more successful in this program if you set up a reward system using things that will motivate you to keep going.

PART THREE

10-WEEK PROGRAM

- CHAPTER 7 -

Week 1: Mindfulness

ORANGE YOU GLAD YOU TRIED IT?

At first, mindfulness felt daunting. I remember thinking it was just meditation and trying to meditate, hoping something would happen inside me, turning on like a switch, and with my newfound enlightenment offering me inner peace, I would stop skin picking. But no, not exactly.

I learned that mindfulness was purposefully paying attention to the present without judging it. In understanding that, I could use it to practice and improve on my goal of lessening my BFRB.

BFRBs often thrive in routine, and I've always been a creature of habit. So instead of trying to force mindfulness into my life in some grand, unfamiliar way, I found a way to weave it into the daily patterns I practiced already.

One place I frequently found myself scanning my skin (leading to skin picking) was right before I hopped on work calls like Zoom meetings. There I'd be. Sitting in front of my laptop, prepping the business matters to discuss for my nonprofit. I'd start feeling excited and nervous. And my fingers would start scanning my skin for some sensory input.

So I came up with a plan.

I started scheduling my Zoom meetings five minutes earlier, just for me. And I'd bring an orange.

For those five minutes, I'd let my senses take over, and I'd experience that orange. The crisp sound of peel fibers tearing. The sharp smell of the rind piercing my nose. The cool juice dripping plump, wet beads down my fingertips. The quenching first bite, squishing around loud and bright like a summer musical. Whichever sense grabbed me first, I focused on it fully. Not only did it help ground me, it kept my hands busy. Then the meeting began with my hands at ease.

And just like that, a new routine was born.

One where I break the orange's skin, not my own.

Lauren McKeaney

You've probably heard of mindfulness, but do you really know what it is? Let's start with a quick quiz to test your knowledge of mindfulness.

MINDFULNESS POP QUIZ

Please check the box next to each statement that you think is **true**.

- ☐ Mindfulness means paying attention in a particular way, on purpose, in the present moment, and nonjudgmentally.
- ☐ You need to clear your mind in order to practice mindfulness.
- ☐ Mindfulness requires you to sit on a cushion with your legs crossed.
- ☐ Mindfulness practice strengthens the neural pathways in your brain (like roads connecting one part of your brain to another), like how physical exercise strengthens your muscles.
- ☐ Mindfulness is a religious practice.
- ☐ When you practice mindfulness, you will feel relaxed.
- ☐ You need to practice mindfulness regularly in order to achieve the full benefits of the practice.
- ☐ Over time, mindfulness practice will help you become more aware of what you are doing, which will help you make better choices.
- ☐ Meditation is the only way to practice mindfulness.
- ☐ Informal mindfulness practices involve doing an everyday activity while bringing attention to one or more of your five senses.

Now, turn to the last page of this chapter for the answers. So, how did you do? Don't worry if you checked off a lot of the wrong ones. This was meant to be kind of tricky, since it listed many of the common misconceptions about mindfulness. Now that you know a little more about what mindfulness is and is **not**, let's practice some mindfulness exercises.

MINDFUL EATING

The first practice we're going to do is an informal practice called mindful eating. Go grab a small piece of food like a raisin, nut, piece of candy, or piece of fruit. Then, before you start eating it, visit www.jkp.com/catalogue/book/9781805018650 or scan the QR code here for guided instructions.

Mindful Eating Inquiry

After each mindfulness practice, it's important to reflect on what you experienced. Please answer the following questions.

What did you observe? (Write out some of the things you noticed about your piece of food.)

....

....

How is this different from how you normally eat?

....

....

What is the point of this? How is mindfully eating going to help manage your BFRB?

....

....

Mindful Matching Exercise

This activity will test your knowledge of how the mindful eating exercise allows you to practice each of the principles of mindfulness. Get three different color pencils, markers, or crayons. Match each mindfulness principle on the left with the statement about mindful eating on the right that is an example of that principle by coloring them in the same color.

Mindfulness principles	Mindful eating
Paying attention on purpose	Every time your mind wanders, bring it back to the present by returning your attention to one of your five senses.
Paying attention in the present moment	Notice any judgment that arises, such as labeling the food as good or bad, and try to find another more descriptive word to use, such as tasty or sour.
Paying attention without judgment	Step out of autopilot by intentionally becoming aware of what you are eating and the process of eating it by tuning into each of your five senses.

What's the Point of Practicing Mindful Eating (or Other Informal Mindfulness Practices)?

Check each box if you'd like to achieve this benefit.

- ☐ By practicing focused attention, you strengthen the brain connections (neural pathways) that help you pay attention. Over time, this makes it easier for you to notice when you're engaging in your BFRB.
- ☐ Being able to focus on the present will help you manage any stress, anxiety, and/or depression that you experience, because often our minds are in the past or future during these unwanted emotional states.
- ☐ Reducing judgment helps you be more accepting of your triggers, urges, your BFRB itself, and yourself for doing the behavior.

OTHER INFORMAL MINDFULNESS PRACTICES

Check the boxes below of any informal practices you'd like to try and add a few of your own.

- ☐ Brushing your teeth
- ☐ Petting your dog, cat, or other pet
- ☐ Taking a walk
- ☐ Sitting outside
- ☐ Doing the dishes
- ☐ Coloring
- ☐ Other: ....

All you have to do for an informal practice is to bring your attention to one or more of your five senses while you're doing the activity.

FORMAL MINDFULNESS PRACTICE: THE BODY SCAN

Although meditation is not the only way to practice mindfulness, it is still one of the best! Traditional mindfulness courses taught by Jon Kabat-Zinn, who we refer to as the grandfather of mindfulness, included 30–45-minute-long meditations. While there are certainly some benefits to a longer meditation, most people don't have that much time to dedicate to a daily practice.

Research shows that a daily meditation practice, even of just a few minutes each day, will help increase focus and concentration, and reduce levels of anxiety and depression.

Visit www.jkp.com/catalogue/book/9781805018650 or scan the QR code here to do your first meditation practice.

Body Scan Inquiry

What did you notice during this meditation?

....

....

How is this exercise different from how you normally relate to your body?

....

....

What is the point of this? How will practicing the body scan meditation help you manage your BFRB?

....

....

What's the Point of Practicing the Body Scan?

Check each box if you'd like to achieve this benefit.

- ☐ Help me learn to direct my attention to the present moment and accept whatever is there, so it is a practice in both awareness and acceptance.
- ☐ Becoming more aware of the sensations in my body will help me become more aware of what triggers me and how I feel these triggers in my body, where I feel my urges, and how my BFRB makes me feel in my body.
- ☐ Acceptance of discomfort in my body is the first step towards accepting an urge to pick or pull, as well as helping me move towards self-acceptance.

DEVELOPING A REGULAR MINDFULNESS PRACTICE

Set a time each day that you can do the body scan meditation so that you can establish a habit of regular practice for the best chance of successfully managing your BFRB and related emotions.

1. What time will you practice each day? ....
2. Set a daily alarm in your phone right now to remind you to practice each day.

3. What do you think might get in the way of you practicing every day? List at least two or three obstacles below:

   ....

   ....

4. What can you do to get around these obstacles so that they don't get in your way?[1]

   ....

   ....

SETTING AN INTENTION FOR YOUR MINDFULNESS PRACTICE

Considering how your BFRB has negatively impacted your life, and your inability to manage it using things you've tried so far, are you willing to try something new that has been proven effective?

☐ Yes
☐ No

If you answered "no," you may not be ready to dive deeper into this workbook right now. And that is okay. But it's important to name this and work on this before proceeding with this workbook. Discuss your concerns with your support team and brainstorm with them about any ways to increase your motivation.

If you answered "yes," that is great! Let's move on! Go ahead and write out a statement identifying when and why you are going to practice mindfulness each day.

Here are some sample intentions:

I will practice mindfulness each day before lunch by doing a body scan meditation and then take my first few bites of lunch mindfully so that I will be more aware of when I'm picking.

I will do a body scan before I go to bed each night, and I will do an informal practice of brushing my teeth mindfully before bed so that I will be able to manage my stress better.

1 If you end up missing a day, **do not** give up on the practice altogether. While it's best to practice daily, it is much better to practice five or six days a week than none.

Now write yours:

....

....

Here are three more steps to help increase the chances of you following your intention. Check each box when you complete the task.

- ☐ Write this intention on a sticky note or index card and place it somewhere you will see it every day as a reminder of your intention.
- ☐ Come up with a small daily reward for practicing mindfulness, such as a piece of candy or watching a favorite show.
- ☐ Share your intention and reward with your support team and remind them of when you want them to check in for reminders and support.

Congratulations, you've completed the Week 1 material. Here are your action steps for the week.

WEEK 1 ACTION STEPS

1. Practice the body scan meditation every day as your formal mindfulness practice.
2. Do an informal mindfulness practice every day, such as brushing your teeth or mindfully eating a few bites of a snack.
3. Log each of these practices in your mindfulness practice log below.
4. Give yourself the rewards you earn.

CHECKING IN WITH YOUR SUPPORT TEAM

When and how will you share your action steps and reward plan with your support people?

....

....

When and how would you like them to check in and support you this week?

....

....

Who can you call, text, or connect with right now to make it more likely that you will seek support this week?

....

....

MINDFULNESS PRACTICE LOG

Formal Practice: Guided Meditation

Date	What I practiced	Thoughts, feelings, and physical sensations that you noticed during the meditation, and how you felt after
Sample	*Body scan*	*I felt anxious at first and it was hard to focus, but by the end I was feeling more relaxed*

Informal Practice: An Activity or Moment that You Bring Mindful Attention to

Date and time	Situation/ activity	What did you notice?	How did you feel?	What did you learn?
Sample	*Brushing my teeth*	*The smell and taste of my toothpaste, the sound of the brushing, feeling it on my teeth*	*Calm*	*I miss a lot when I'm not paying attention*

ANSWERS TO MINDFULNESS POP QUIZ

The following statements are true. The rest are false.

- Mindfulness means paying attention in a particular way, on purpose, in the present moment, and nonjudgmentally.
- Mindfulness practice strengthens the neural pathways in your brain (like roads connecting one part of your brain to another), like how physical exercise strengthens your muscles.
- You need to practice mindfulness regularly in order to achieve the full benefits of the practice.
- Over time, mindfulness practice will help you become more aware of what you are doing, which will help you make better choices.
- Informal mindfulness practices involve doing an everyday activity while bringing attention to one or more of your five senses.

- CHAPTER 8 -

Week 2: Tracking

FOR THE RECORD

I thought I knew what tracking was. And honestly? I wasn't into it.

I was already painfully aware of how often I skin picked. Did I really need a written record to remind me? It just seemed like a fast track to feeling worse.

But bleeding every day, I was willing to give it a try.

At first, it felt weird, like I was just jotting down all my mistakes. But the more I logged, the more I saw a pattern. And the more patterns I saw, the more I understood my BFRB.

Reframing tracking as my own personal research project, not a list of slip-ups but a tool to help me move forward, changed everything. Instead of feeling powerless, I felt proactive. I had pages of information to look back on, data, and prepped with that knowledge, I could actually do something about it.

From reviewing my logs, I learned that I scanned the sides of my thighs for skin irregularities as I pulled my pants down to use the bathroom. I had done this a zillion times before but hadn't put together that that action led to skin picking until logging.

Primed with this knowledge, I decided to try holding a fidget while in the bathroom to keep one hand busy. And it helped.

Thanks to the log.

Remember, tracking (like life) doesn't have to be perfect. Just get pen to paper. And for my filled-out log example, head to https://pickingme.org/skinpickinglog.

Lauren McKeaney

Week 1 Check-In

Before we dive into the Week 2 material, let's check in to reflect on how Week 1 went.

Have you been practicing mindfulness regularly?

- ☐ Yes, I practiced every single day this week.
- ☐ Yes, I practiced four to six times this week.
- ☐ Not quite, but I practiced one to three times this week.
- ☐ No, I did not practice this week.

How have you felt this week?

- ☐ Calm
- ☐ Anxious
- ☐ Bored
- ☐ Indifferent
- ☐ Relaxed
- ☐ Distracted
- ☐ Focused
- ☐ Sleepy
- ☐ Energized
- ☐ Other: ....

Have you noticed any of the following benefits in your life this week (even if just a little bit)?

- ☐ I'm more aware of when I'm doing my BFRB.
- ☐ I feel a little less anxious.
- ☐ I am not getting frustrated as often.
- ☐ I am more grateful for things that are going well.
- ☐ When I get upset, I can calm down more quickly.
- ☐ I'm sleeping better at night.
- ☐ I feel more rested during the day.
- ☐ I'm doing my BFRB a little bit less.
- ☐ When I notice I'm doing the BFRB, I can stop more quickly.
- ☐ Other: ....

How is your support system working?

- ☐ Great, no changes needed at all! I feel supported and held accountable by them.
- ☐ Pretty good, but it could be better.
- ☐ Okay, but it could use some changes.
- ☐ Not very good.
- ☐ What support system?

If you selected anything other than the first option, no problem. Stop here. Go back to Chapter 6 and see what changes you can make to improve your support system. Below, write the steps that you will take right away to make sure that you get the support you need.

....

....

FOCUSED VS UNFOCUSED

Many people with BFRBs are not aware that they are even doing the behavior some or all of the time. This is referred to as **unfocused** picking or pulling. There are usually times when you are looking at the spot or hair that you're picking or pulling, either in the mirror or directly at the skin or hair. This is called **focused** picking or pulling.

Which do you do more often?

- ☐ I'm usually focused on the behavior while I'm doing it.
- ☐ I'm usually not focused on the behavior while I'm doing it.
- ☐ I engage equally in focused and unfocused behaviors.
- ☐ I don't know which I do more often.

Unfocused picking or pulling often leads to extensive damage to the skin and/or hair and can take up hours of one's day. Most interventions are not effective when the individual doesn't know when they're doing the behavior.

We started with mindfulness training to gain awareness of when the behavior is being done. In this chapter, we'll look more closely at when, where, and why you do the behavior through tracking. First, though, we will do another meditation practice to get grounded to the present moment.

MINDFUL BREATHING

To continue building on your mindfulness practice, we're going to try another meditation today called mindful breathing. Visit www.jkp.com/catalogue/book/9781805018650 or scan the QR code here to listen and follow along with the guided meditation.

Mindful Breathing Inquiry

What did you notice during this meditation?

How is this exercise different from how you normally breathe?

What is the point of this? How do you think practicing this meditation will help you manage your BFRB?

TRACKING

Becoming aware of when, where, and why you do your BFRB is crucial in figuring out which tools are going to work the best for you. Don't worry—you'll only need to track for one week. Dr Charles Mansueto, a BFRB expert in the Washington DC area, and his colleagues created a comprehensive model for behavioral treatment of BFRBs in 1999 called ComB.

This treatment model provides a good framework for what to track in order to develop an individualized treatment plan. ComB uses the acronym "SCAMP" to remind you of what to monitor.

- **Sensory**: What do you notice using your five senses before, during, and after you do the behavior? What sensory need may this behavior be fulfilling?

- **Cognitive**: What thoughts are going through your head before, during, and after you do the behavior? How might these thoughts impact you and the behavior?
- **Affective**: What emotions do you notice before, during, and after you do the behavior? How might these emotions contribute to or reinforce the behaviors?
- **Motoric**: Is the behavior done without any awareness, as simply a motor (automatic) movement of the arm, hand, and fingers? How aware are you of where your hand is resting (or moving) when you start and exactly how and where it moves?
- **Place (environment)**: Where do you do the behavior? Is anything in your environment a trigger for you, such as a mirror or the armrest of a coach seat that means when your arm is on it, it is near your face or head?

Why Should I Track?

Some of the benefits of tracking are listed below. Check any that you're interested in gaining.

- ☐ Self-monitoring has been shown to be the most effective way to increase awareness of BFRBs.
- ☐ Increased awareness reduces future episodes of the behavior.
- ☐ It can also help reduce the behavior in the moment by bringing awareness to it.
- ☐ While tracking, sometimes people will do the behavior less because they don't want to have to write it down.
- ☐ Tracking will help you understand what needs are being met by your BFRB so that you can find another way to meet those needs.
- ☐ The better you understand why you're doing the behavior, the less shame you will feel about it.
- ☐ If you know when you're doing the behavior, you can plan to use certain strategies before or during the times that you're more likely to do them.
- ☐ If you know where you're doing the behavior, you can place strategies in those places to remind you to use them.

Tracking Categories

I recommend starting with using the tracking log at the end of this chapter or making sure that all the same categories are included in whatever else you use to track.

If you decide to make your own log on your phone or another device, please check off each category after you add it:

- ☐ Date/time
- ☐ Activity/situation
- ☐ Strength of urge (1–10) and efforts to resist (1–10)
- ☐ Sensory
- ☐ Cognitive
- ☐ Affective
- ☐ Motoric
- ☐ Place/environment

Obstacles with Tracking

Tracking is not all that difficult to do, but many find that it's **very** difficult to keep up with.

Below are some common obstacles to tracking. Check each that you think could be a problem for you:

- ☐ Forgetting to track.
- ☐ Not wanting to take the time to track.
- ☐ Not having the sheet when you need it.
- ☐ Not wanting to stop what you're doing to track.
- ☐ Feeling upset with yourself for doing the behavior and embarrassed to write about it.
- ☐ Not wanting anyone to see what you write on your log.
- ☐ Giving up because it takes too long.
- ☐ Not wanting to bring awareness to your BFRB—thinking that if you bring awareness to it, it will bother you more.
- ☐ Feeling guilty/defeated/upset at noticing your BFRB so much.
- ☐ Thinking that you pick/pull everywhere and everything triggers you, so what's the point in tracking?
- ☐ Thinking you know all your triggers, so what's the point in tracking?
- ☐ Other: ....

Overcoming Obstacles to Tracking

Below are some tips to help you be successful with the tracking. Check any that you will use:

- ☐ Make several copies of the tracking log and put one (and a pen or pencil) in every place you can think of that you might pick or pull (e.g., on your bedside table, bathroom counter, kitchen counter, desk, coffee table, or side table in living room, etc.).
- ☐ Take a picture of the tracking log so you'll have it on your phone as a reference if you don't have it with you.
- ☐ Visit www.jkp.com/catalogue/book/9781805018650 or scan the QR code here to download a digital version of the tracking log.
- ☐ Download an app to track the BFRB, like TrichStop, Skin-Pick, or Keen2 HabitAware.
- ☐ Think of yourself as a researcher gathering data, and the more data the better!
- ☐ Remember, you only need to track for one week.
- ☐ Approach this with curiosity, as you are discovering all that you can about your behavior.

WEEK 2 ACTION STEPS

1. Do a mindful breathing meditation every day.
2. Choose a different informal mindfulness practice to do daily.
3. Start tracking your BFRB as many times as you can each day using the tracking log at the end of this chapter or a digital version of it.
4. Use the reward chart below to track the completion of these goals. Give yourself either a daily reward for completing at least two of the goals or a weekly reward for completing at least 10 goals.
5. Check in with your support team to share these goals and your reward plan, and review when they will check in with you this week.

My Reward Chart

Goal	Mon	Tue	Wed	Thu	Fri	Sat	Sun
Mindful breathing meditation							
Informal mindfulness practice							
Tracking (at least once a day)							

CHECKING IN WITH YOUR SUPPORT TEAM

When and how will you share your action steps and reward plan with your support people?

....

....

When and how would you like them to check in and support you this week?

....

....

Who can you call, text, or connect with right now to make it more likely that you will seek support this week?

....

....

Reminders

✓ This work often brings up a lot of emotions, which can be draining and hard to keep up with.

✓ That's why it's so important to be kind to yourself and reach out for support from others throughout this process.

✓ You've got this.

✓ Just keep taking one step at a time and hopping back up every time you stumble.

Tracking Log

Date and time	Activity/ situation: What were you doing before the behavior started or while you were doing it?	Strength of urge (rate 0–10): Did you try to resist the urge? If so, how and what was the outcome?	Sensory: What sensations did you notice before you started? During? Now?	Cognitive: What thoughts were going through your head before? During? Now?	Affective: How were you feeling before you started? During? Now?	Motoric: How aware were you of doing the behavior (rate 0–10, with 10 being completely aware)?	Place: Where are you? If home, where exactly are you sitting or leaning? Any other environmental triggers?

- CHAPTER 9 -

Week 3: Sensory Strategies

SENSORY SITUATIONS

When I first got my driver's license, I got into a car accident because of skin picking.

I didn't tell anyone that, though. Instead, I said I was putting on eyeliner in the visor mirror when I rear-ended a car at a traffic light. That sounded better. More understandable. (Right?)

But the truth? The visor had originally been down to block the sun. I tried to look past it, to focus on the road, but then I saw it. A tight, textured scab on my face, reflected in the tiny mirror.

And just like that, I was sucked in. My fingers moved before my brain could stop them, drawn to the imperfection I suddenly couldn't ignore. The need to fix it took over. I forgot I was driving.

And I crashed.

That moment exemplifies how dangerous mirrors were for my BFRB.

When I understood what a powerful visual trigger mirrors were for my BFRB, I realized I needed to do something in my car to limit their use and prevent skin picking.

So, I started taping my car's visor mirror shut with washi tape.

It was a small, simple thing. But it worked. The tape was gentle enough that I could pull the visor mirror down if I really needed it, but for the most part, I didn't. Maybe I just didn't want to go through the hassle of taping it back up again. Either way, it kept the visor up. It kept me out of the mirror. And it kept me focused on the road.

Whether vision, sound, touch, smell, or taste, sensory triggers alert me to areas of my body that I feel the need to explore further. They are part of my skin picking experience, during as well as after.

Becoming aware of my sensory experience and triggers, and developing strategies to manage them, has made life with my BFRB easier.

Lauren McKeaney

Week 2 Check-In

Have you been practicing mindfulness regularly?

- ☐ Yes, I practiced every single day this week.
- ☐ Yes, I practiced four to six times this week.
- ☐ Not quite, but I practiced one to three times this week.
- ☐ No, I did not practice this week.

How have you felt this week?

- ☐ Calm
- ☐ Anxious
- ☐ Bored
- ☐ Indifferent
- ☐ Relaxed
- ☐ Distracted
- ☐ Focused
- ☐ Sleepy
- ☐ Energized
- ☐ Other: ....

Have you noticed any of the following benefits in your life this week (even if just a little bit)?

- ☐ I'm more aware of when I'm doing my BFRB.
- ☐ I feel a little less anxious.
- ☐ I am not getting frustrated as often.
- ☐ I am more grateful for things that are going well.
- ☐ When I get upset, I can calm down more quickly.
- ☐ I'm sleeping better at night.
- ☐ I feel more rested during the day.
- ☐ I'm doing my BFRB a little bit less.
- ☐ When I notice I'm doing the BFRB, I can stop more quickly.
- ☐ Other: ....

How is your support system working?

- ☐ Great, no changes needed at all! I feel supported and held accountable by them.

- ☐ Pretty good, but it could be better.
- ☐ Okay, but it could use some changes.
- ☐ Not very good.
- ☐ What support system?

If you selected anything other than the first option, please go back to Chapter 6 and see what changes you can make to improve your support system. Below, write the steps that you will take right away to make sure that you get the support you need.

SENSORY CUES MEDITATION

To begin Week 3, we're going to do a meditation to help identify sensory cues or triggers. Visit www.jkp.com/catalogue/book/9781805018650 or scan the QR code here to begin the meditation.

Sensory Cues Meditation Inquiry

What did you notice during this meditation?

How is this exercise different from how you normally pay attention to your senses?

What is the point of this? How do you think practicing this meditation will help you manage your BFRB?

IDENTIFYING SENSORY CUES

Moving on... now, take some time to answer the following questions to help you identify the specific triggers or cues that lead to you picking or pulling.

What visual characteristics do you look for when choosing which hair to pull or which spot to pick? (E.g., darker hair, red spot.)

....

....

Which textures do you feel for when deciding which hair to pull or spot to pick? (E.g., thicker hair, raised spot on skin.)

....

....

How are your senses stimulated or soothed by the behavior? (E.g., some people feel calmed by feeling smooth skin, while others say that putting a hair follicle in their mouth feels stimulating.)

....

....

What sensations do you notice while you're doing the behavior?

....

....

What sensations do you notice after you've done the behavior?

....

....

Are there sensations you're trying to achieve? (E.g., symmetrical looking eyebrows, smooth skin.)

....

....

Trying Out Common Sensory Strategies

Put a checkmark next to any of these strategies that you'd like to try (even if you've tried them before).

Substitution strategies:

- ☐ String
- ☐ Knotted dental floss
- ☐ Doll or wig hair
- ☐ Bubble wrap
- ☐ Burlap
- ☐ Paint brush bristles

Soothe or stimulate your senses:

- ☐ Look at pictures of hair follicles (sense of sight)
- ☐ Watch YouTube videos of picking or pulling (sight)
- ☐ Koosh balls (touch)
- ☐ Tangle toys (touch)
- ☐ Soft brush (touch)
- ☐ Smooth stone (touch)
- ☐ Feather (touch)
- ☐ Pipe cleaner (touch)
- ☐ Head massager (touch)
- ☐ Fabric swatches (touch)
- ☐ Acupressure rings (touch)
- ☐ Items that make popping sounds, like silly putty (sound)
- ☐ Bubble wrap (sound and touch)
- ☐ Scented lotion (smell)
- ☐ Candle (smell)
- ☐ Bath bomb (smell and touch)
- ☐ Chew gum (taste and touch)
- ☐ Peppermints or other candy (taste)
- ☐ Sunflower seeds (taste, touch, and sound)
- ☐ Dry spaghetti (taste, touch, and sound)
- ☐ Gummy bears (taste and touch)

Engage in healthy grooming and skin care routines:

- ☐ Hand cream

- ☐ Body lotion
- ☐ Facial masks
- ☐ Face lotion
- ☐ Cortisone cream for itching
- ☐ Antibiotic ointment for cuts or scabs
- ☐ Acne medication
- ☐ Brush hair
- ☐ Shower daily
- ☐ Start new skincare routines for morning and/or night

Treat yourself to something special:

- ☐ Manicure
- ☐ Pedicure
- ☐ Facial
- ☐ Massage

Add don't subtract:

- ☐ Instead of evening things out or seeking symmetry by doing more damage, use cosmetics to cover up the damage.
- ☐ Add color to areas that are missing hair (e.g., eye liner to hide missing lashes or brows, colored hair powder or spray to fill in bald spots).

Developing Your Own Unique Strategies

Keeping in mind your own particular sensory cues, identify specific strategies you will use in each category.

Visual/sense of sight

Strategies for blocking visual cues:

- ☐ Cover mirror with fabric or paper.
- ☐ Stand further from mirror.

Other ways to reduce access to mirrors:

- ☐ Dim lights in your bedroom and bathroom.
- ☐ Cover your problem areas with clothing or Band-Aids.
- ☐ Wear a hat, headband, or other head covering.

Other ways to make it harder to see your skin or hair:

- ☐ Other: ....

Other visual strategies:

- ☐ Add instead of subtract.
- ☐ Use makeup to cover problem areas.
- ☐ Put on a face mask.
- ☐ Pictures of hair follicles.
- ☐ YouTube videos.
- ☐ Other: ....

Texture/sense of touch

Block tactile cues:

- ☐ Wear gloves.
- ☐ Put Band-Aids on fingers.
- ☐ Cover head with a hat or headband.
- ☐ Put hair in a ponytail.
- ☐ Other: ....

Other ways to get tactile stimulation:

- ☐ Wash and/or brush hair or skin.
- ☐ Use a facial scrub or mask.
- ☐ Use a massage brush.
- ☐ Rub a smooth stone or soft blanket.
- ☐ Use an acupuncture ring.
- ☐ Play with a fidget or tangle toy.
- ☐ Pull hairs from a soft brush, doll, or wig.
- ☐ Other: ....

Ways to soothe and heal the hair and/or skin:

- ☐ Use hand, body, or face lotion.
- ☐ Start a new skincare routine.
- ☐ Try a new shampoo and conditioner.
- ☐ Use a hair or face mask.
- ☐ Use medicated cream to treat acne, scarring, or open wounds.

- ☐ Use hair-growth serum.
- ☐ Wash your skin or hair.
- ☐ Get a manicure.
- ☐ Get a pedicure.
- ☐ Other: ....

Smell, sound, and taste

What other sensory strategies would you like to try?

- ☐ Items that make popping sound, like silly putty (sound)
- ☐ Bubble wrap (sound and touch)
- ☐ Scented lotion (smell)
- ☐ Candle (smell)
- ☐ Bath bomb (smell and touch)
- ☐ Chew gum (taste and touch)
- ☐ Peppermints or other candy (taste)
- ☐ Sunflower seeds (taste, touch, and sound)
- ☐ Dry spaghetti (taste, touch, and sound)
- ☐ Gummy bears (taste and touch)

Putting It All Together: My Sensory Plan

My sensory cues	My sensory strategies

REWARD PLAN

1. Choose three strategies from the above to focus on over the next week.
2. Set up systems to make sure you will use these strategies (e.g., reminders, putting items out now).

3. Set up rewards for successfully **trying** the strategies, whether they are successful in reducing the behavior or not. At least you tried, and that matters!
4. You can choose a daily or weekly reward and give yourself the reward even if you don't do the strategy perfectly (e.g., every day or every time). You just want to reward any steps in the right direction.
5. **Reward ideas**: Candy, Starbucks, manicure, dinner out, new shirt, download a song, new game, new book, rent a movie, go out with a friend, etc.
6. **Example of good reward plan**: If I use a strategy a total of 15 times over the next week, I will get a manicure.
7. Put a checkmark, smiley face, or small sticker on each day that you use the strategy.

MY REWARD PLAN

If I use . . . . (2 or 15—these numbers are samples of good targets to strive for, but you can enter any number you'd like) strategies per . . . . (day or week) then I will earn: . . . .

Strategy	Mon	Tue	Wed	Thu	Fri	Sat	Sun

WEEK 3 ACTION STEPS

1. Practice your first three sensory strategies every day over the next week.
2. Put a checkmark or small sticker in the box each time you **use one of the strategies**.
3. You get a point or checkmark regardless of whether you pick or pull or not, because we are rewarding what you have control over.
4. Continue your daily formal and informal mindfulness practice as best you can.

Reminders

- ✓ It's normal to get off track with your mindfulness practice or other strategies in this book.
- ✓ Every time you notice that you are not being mindful, gently guide your mind back to the present, like you would guide a cute puppy who you were training.
- ✓ Being gentle with yourself is the best way to help you create new healthier habits.

- CHAPTER 10 -

Week 4: Thinking and Feeling Strategies

CHALLENGING THOUGHTS AND FEELINGS FOR THE WIN

Thoughts thoroughly impacted my skin picking.

It was overwhelming to think about living like this forever. Thinking my skin had to be perfect and smooth. Thinking everyone was looking at my skin and thinking I was gross. Or thinking that even if I picked a little, I lost.

But when I started questioning these thoughts, digging into them (not my skin), I found some relief. When I gave myself room to interpret them instead of just reacting, I started to manage my BFRB in a way that actually helped.

For example, suppose I saw the crust of a healing scab in a mirror briefly. I would first be met with the urge to remove it. In that case, I'd remind myself my profession was not dermatology, and bodies have been capable of shedding a scab without my assistance since forever.

Along with thoughts, feelings fueled my skin picking. And feeling like I'd accomplished something, completed it, was a big motivator.

It felt like an immense success or win if I got the scab off fully (and in the right way). Or if I squeezed a mound and something projected out of a pore and splattered on my mirror, I'd feel like YES, I'd won!

Incorporating a finger activity that kept my hands busy and mind focused, with an end goal (something to accomplish), offered me an alternative to one of the feelings my skin picking served.

So I had to find another way to channel that need for accomplishment, one that didn't involve my skin.

Enter: the friendship bracelet.

Before Taylor Swift brought them back, us '90s kids rocked them religiously, trading them like currency in class. Those colorful, knotted strings wrapped our wrists and ankles like beautiful badges of honor. Proof of friendships formed as summers spilled into school time.

And now? I've resurrected this nostalgic pastime and incorporated it as a skin picking management strategy to prevent me scanning while watching TV. I just keep a bracelet to work on tied to the remote for my TV, always ready to go.

The moment I go to watch something, I have an automatic activity waiting for me, one that keeps my hands busy and mind engaged. Instead of picking, I'm braiding. Knot by knot, pattern by pattern achieved, I get to watch something progress and grow. (Like me.)

Lauren McKeaney

Week 3 Check-In

Have you been practicing mindfulness regularly?

- ☐ Yes, I practiced every single day this week.
- ☐ Yes, I practiced four to six times this week.
- ☐ Not quite, but I practiced one to three times this week.
- ☐ No, I did not practice this week.

How have you felt this week?

- ☐ Calm
- ☐ Anxious
- ☐ Bored
- ☐ Indifferent
- ☐ Relaxed
- ☐ Distracted
- ☐ Focused
- ☐ Sleepy
- ☐ Energized
- ☐ Other: ....

Have you noticed any of the following benefits in your life this week (even if just a little bit)?

- ☐ I'm more aware of when I'm doing my BFRB.
- ☐ I feel a little less anxious.

- ☐ I am not getting frustrated as often.
- ☐ I am more grateful for things that are going well.
- ☐ When I get upset, I can calm down more quickly.
- ☐ I'm sleeping better at night.
- ☐ I feel more rested during the day.
- ☐ I'm doing my BFRB a little bit less.
- ☐ When I notice I'm doing the BFRB, I can stop more quickly.
- ☐ Other: ....

How is your support system working?

- ☐ Great, no changes needed at all! I feel supported and held accountable by them.
- ☐ Pretty good, but it could be better.
- ☐ Okay, but it could use some changes.
- ☐ Not very good.
- ☐ What support system?

If you selected anything other than the first option, please go back to Chapter 6 and see what changes you can make to improve your support system. Below, write the steps that you will take right away to make sure that you get the support you need.

....

....

In this chapter, you will learn which thoughts and feelings make your BFRB worse and strategies to manage them in a better way. Let's get started with identifying the thoughts (also known as cognitions) that are related to your BFRB. We call these cognitive cues.

COGNITIVE CUES (AKA TRIGGERING THOUGHTS)

Challenge yourself to come up with at least two thoughts for each of these categories.

What thoughts do you have before you do the behavior? (E.g., My skin needs to be smooth. This hair needs to go.)

1. ....

2. ....

3. ....

What thoughts do you have while you're doing the behavior? (E.g., I'll just pull one more. I can't stop.)

1. ....

2. ....

3. ....

What thoughts do you have after doing the behavior? (E.g., What's wrong with me? I'm such a failure.)

1. ....

2. ....

3. ....

What thoughts or beliefs do you have about the consequence of the behavior? (E.g., I look terrible. Everyone will notice this spot on my face.)

1. ....

2. ....

3. ....

What thoughts or beliefs do you have about your ability to control the behavior? (E.g., I will never be able to stop doing this.)

1. ....

2. ....

3. ....

What thoughts or beliefs do you have about bumps in the road? (E.g., I've failed again. There's no point in keeping trying anymore.)

1. ....

2. ....

3. ....

Now that you've gotten a lot of thoughts about your BFRB out of your head, you may feel some feelings that aren't the most pleasant, because our thoughts and feelings are often closely connected.

Here's a list of some common feelings that teens with BFRBs feel. Choose a different color for each of the emotions that you feel when thinking about your BFRB and color the name of that emotion in that color. If you never feel that emotion when you think of your BFRB, you can leave it white.

- ★ Ashamed
- ★ Embarrassed
- ★ Angry
- ★ Sad
- ★ Alone
- ★ Worried
- ★ Frustrated
- ★ Hurt
- ★ Lonely
- ★ Depressed
- ★ Anxious
- ★ Nervous
- ★ Jealous
- ★ Scared
- ★ Hopeful
- ★ Relieved
- ★ Calm
- ★ Relaxed
- ★ Happy

Now that you've created your emotion legend, go back to the thoughts you wrote above, and put a checkmark next to each thought in the color of each emotion that you feel when you say that thought in your head (or aloud if you prefer). Notice how your thoughts impact how you feel.

The good news about thoughts is that we do have some control over them. We cannot stop a thought from popping into our head, but we can challenge the thought to take away some of its power or change the channel to help us not focus so much on it. The cognitive strategies below are designed to help you do this.

Cognitive Strategies

Circle the number next to each strategy that you'd like to try, even if you've tried it before.

1. **Mindfulness/thought watching**: A thought is just a thought, not a fact or the truth. Think of it as just a temporary mental event that will pass on its own, and just let it be as it is. You can practice a thought watching meditation to visualize your thoughts moving past you without grabbing hold of them and giving them more meaning. Visit www.jkp.com/catalogue/book/9781805018650 or scan the QR code above to do a thought watching meditation now.

2. **Thought watching meditation inquiry**:
   - What did you notice while doing this meditation?

     ....

     ....

   - How is this different from how you normally pay attention to your thoughts?

     ....

     ....

   - How could this be helpful for you, especially with regard to your BFRB?

     ....

     ....

3. **Thought challenging**:
   - **Cognitive distortions** are unhelpful ways of thinking that can make you feel worse about yourself or a situation. It's like when your brain tricks you into believing something is way more negative or extreme than it really is. These thoughts can make small problems seem huge or make you feel like everything is going wrong, even when it's not.
   - For example: You might think, "If I mess up once, I'm a total failure," but that's your brain jumping to an unfair conclusion. Or you might think, "My friend didn't reply right away, so they must be mad at me," when in reality, they could just be busy.
   - When you notice these patterns, you can challenge them to see the situation more clearly and feel better.

Here's a list of cognitive distortions that teens and young adults with BFRBs commonly use. Put a checkmark by each one that sounds like something you have thought.

☐ **All-or-nothing thinking (aka black and white thinking)**:
   - Seeing situations in extremes, without recognizing any middle ground.

- ▹ Believing that if you can't completely stop your BFRB, then you're a failure.
- ▹ For example: "I pulled out one hair, so I might as well pull out the rest."

☐ **Catastrophizing**:
- ▹ Expecting the worst possible outcome.
- ▹ For example: "If I pick at my skin, it will never heal and everyone will judge me."

☐ **Overgeneralization**:
- ▹ A single negative event is seen as a never-ending pattern of defeat.
- ▹ For example: "I picked once today, so I'll never be able to stop."

☐ **Mental filtering**:
- ▹ Focusing only on the negative aspects of your behavior while ignoring any progress.
- ▹ For example: "I haven't picked my skin in a week, but since I did it today, all that progress is meaningless."

☐ **Disqualifying the positive**:
- ▹ Dismissing positive steps or improvements.
- ▹ For example: "Sure, I haven't pulled my hair for days, but it doesn't count because I'll probably do it again soon."

☐ **Jumping to conclusions**:
- ▹ Making assumptions about what others think or about future events without evidence.
- ▹ For example: "Everyone notices and is disgusted by my skin picking."

☐ **Magnification or minimization**:
- ▹ Exaggerating the importance of your BFRB episodes or minimizing your ability to manage them.
- ▹ For example: "This is the worst thing ever!" or "It's not that bad; I don't need to do anything to stop."

☐ **Shoulds or musts**:
- ▹ Imposing strict rules about what you should or must do.
- ▹ For example: "I should be able to stop pulling my hair by now."

- ☐ **Labeling**:
  - ▹ Assigning negative labels to yourself based on your behavior.
  - ▹ For example: "I'm disgusting because I pick my skin."

- ☐ **Emotional reasoning**:
  - ▹ Believing that how you feel reflects reality.
  - ▹ For example: "I feel out of control, so I must actually be out of control."

- ☐ **Blaming**:
  - ▹ Blaming other people or circumstances for your behavior, which can prevent personal accountability.
  - ▹ For example: "I wouldn't bite my nails if school wasn't so stressful."

- ☐ **Personalization**:
  - ▹ Blaming yourself for things outside of your control or believing that your BFRB defines your worth.
  - ▹ For example: "It's my fault I can't stop pulling, and that makes me a failure."

- ☐ **Minimizing achievements**:
  - ▹ Downplaying successes in managing the behavior.
  - ▹ For example: "Sure, I managed not to pick for a week, but it wasn't that hard, so it doesn't count."

- ☐ **Fortune telling**:
  - ▹ Predicting that you will fail in your attempts to stop without any real evidence.
  - ▹ For example: "No matter what I do, I'll never be able to stop pulling."

Here's a completed example of the thought challenging worksheet for you to check out before you try this yourself.

Thought challenging example

What is the situation that is bothering you?

Seeing a hair that isn't like the others.

What thoughts are popping into your mind about it? What are you worried will happen?

This one shouldn't be here. It needs to go. I should just pull it so I can go back to focusing on my homework. If I don't pull it, I'll never be able to relax.

Circle the "hot thought," the one that makes you feel the worst.

How true does this thought **feel** (0–100%)? *95%*

List the evidence that suggests that this thought is true.

Whenever I feel this way, I have to pull it to feel better.
Until I pull it, I won't be able to focus on anything else.
I'm feeling really stressed and need to get back to work.

List the evidence that suggests that this thought is **not** true or not completely true.

If I pull one hair, I will probably want to pull more, and then I'll be mad at myself for pulling.

It's possible that if I try using mindfulness skills with my homework, I can gently redirect my attention back to my homework every time I start to think about pulling.

I will feel anxious at first, but my anxiety may go down over time as I keep focusing back on my homework and see that I'm doing it. If not, I can pull then.

Identify the cognitive distortions or thinking errors that are making you believe that this thought is true.

Fortune telling
Should or musts

Using logic and facts, how true do you think it actually is (0–100%)? *55%*

Develop a balanced belief, taking into account the work completed above.

I don't know for sure that I won't be able to focus on my work if I don't pull this hair, so even though I'm feeling stressed and want to pull, I can try to resist and see if I can redirect my attention back to homework. If I'm able to do it for one minute, then I'll try for another minute.

Now that you know how to do thought challenging, it's time to try your own. Pick something that is bothering you right now. You can choose something related to your BFRB or something that is stressing you out or bothering you even if it's not about your BFRB.

Thought challenging exercise

What is a situation that is bothering you?

....

....

What thoughts are popping into your mind about it? What are you worried will happen?

....

....

Circle the "hot thought," the one that makes you feel the worst.

How true does this thought **feel** (0–100%)? ....

List the evidence that suggests that this thought is true.

....

....

List the evidence that suggests that this thought is **not** true or not completely true.

....

....

Identify the cognitive distortions or thinking errors that are making you believe that this thought is true.

....

....

Using logic and facts, how true do you think it actually is (0–100%)? ....

Develop a balanced belief, taking into account the work completed above.

....

....

How do you feel now that you've completed the thought challenging exercise?

....

....

This is just one of the cognitive strategies that you can try this week. Here are a few more.

- **Test your beliefs**: Do experiments to test your beliefs. For example, to test the belief "This pimple won't go away unless I pick it," leave it alone for three days to see what happens. Gather data by observing it or even taking pictures but not touching it at all.
- **Education**: Learn more about normal hair/skin growth and the healing process, and the nature of BFRBs, to help challenge distorted beliefs about what will happen if you leave it alone vs continuing to mess with it.
- **Turn an unhelpful thought into a helpful thought**: List unhelpful thoughts and then for each one think about what similar thought would be more helpful to believe. Try this one now below.

Unhelpful thoughts	Helpful thoughts
I need to pick this scab to make my skin smooth.	*Picking will temporarily make it smoother, but then it will scab over again, and then over time, I will develop scars, so it's best to just let it heal now.*

Now that you've tried several cognitive strategies, choose one or two cognitive strategies to try this week.

My Cognitive Strategies

1. ....

2. ....

Now that you know how to identify and manage your thoughts related to your BFRB, let's start working on your emotions. Affect is just another word for an emotion or feeling.

AFFECTIVE (AKA EMOTIONAL) CUES

Answer the following questions to help identify your emotions related to your BFRB.

What emotions do you experience before, during, and after you do the behavior?

....

....

Do you ever feel an increasing sense of tension or an urge to pick or pull? If so, what does that feel like?

....

....

Do you ever feel good, satisfied, or relieved after you do the behavior? If so, how long do these feelings usually last? What happens after they fade?

....

....

Do you ever feel disappointed, angry, or frustrated with the behavior?

....

....

Do others make comments, criticize, or seem disappointed that you're doing the behavior? If so, how does this make you feel?

....

....

Does the behavior affect how you feel about yourself? If so, how?

....

....

Affective Strategies

Put a checkmark next to any of the strategies listed below that sound like they might be helpful for you. Then you'll choose one or two to practice this week.

- ☐ Practice mindfulness daily to help manage your emotions through acceptance. Sit with the feelings and let them be as they are. Often our resistance to our feelings makes them much stronger. Pain × Resistance = Suffering
- ☐ **Use relaxation techniques**: Progressive muscle relaxation (PMR)—tensing and then relaxing each muscle in your body one at a time, starting at your feet and moving all the way up to your face; deep breathing—breathing from your diaphragm slowly; visualization—close your eyes and imagine being in a very relaxing place, using as much detail with each of your senses as you can.
- ☐ **Engage in physical exercise or hobbies that stimulate your mind and/or body**: Playing a sport, cooking, running, yoga, pushups, walking, coloring, scrapbooking, beading, etc.
- ☐ **Spend time doing things you enjoy**: Read, see friends, play a video game, go out to eat, watch a movie, volunteer, go to religious services/youth group, listen to music, etc.
- ☐ **Accomplish something**: Complete your homework, clean your room, take a shower, get dressed, make breakfast, etc.
- ☐ **Try something new**: Stretch yourself out of your comfort zone by trying a new food, TV show, type of exercise, restaurant, etc.
- ☐ **Do something creative**: Write, draw, dance, paint, sing, build, etc.
- ☐ Talk to a friend or family member about your feelings, and ask them to just listen and provide validation and empathy rather than advice.

- ☐ Write about your feelings in a journal or notes app on your phone to get them out of your head and process them.
- ☐ See a therapist and/or a psychiatrist to receive additional help with managing your emotions.
- ☐ Other ideas that you have to help manage your feelings: ....

My Affective Strategies

From the list above or any other ideas you have, choose one or two affective strategies that you'd like to try this week.

1. ....

2. ....

Now it's time to put your strategies for the week into your reward chart.

MY REWARD PLAN

If I use .... (2 or 15) strategies per .... (day or week) then I will earn: ....

Strategy	Mon	Tue	Wed	Thu	Fri	Sat	Sun

WEEK 4 ACTION STEPS

1. Practice one to three cognitive or affective strategies every day over the next week.
2. Put a checkmark or small sticker in the box each time you **use one of the strategies**.

3. You get a point or checkmark regardless of whether you pick or pull or not, because we are rewarding what you have control over.
4. Continue your daily formal and informal mindfulness practice as best you can. Remember that it's normal to get off track. Every time you notice that you are not being mindful, gently guide your mind back to the present, like you would guide a cute puppy who you were training.

CHECKING IN WITH YOUR SUPPORT TEAM

When and how will you share your action steps and reward plan with your support people?

....

....

When and how would you like them to check in and support you this week?

....

....

Who can you call, text, or connect with right now to make it more likely that you will seek support this week?

....

....

Reminders

✓ As the weeks go by and you keep learning new strategies, it can feel exciting and hopeful but it can also feel stressful and overwhelming to keep up with all of your new skills.

✓ It's okay if you mess up some days (or even weeks); just remember that your greatest strength is your ability to get back up and start trying again.

- CHAPTER 11 -

Week 5: Movement and Place Strategies

INSIDE SHADES AREN'T SHADY

Sometimes my fingers felt like they had a mind of their own.

If I was excited or nervous, my hands would start to automatically wander across my skin, without me telling them to. Often I'd only become aware I'd picked because of the blood on my hands. Or someone pointing it out.

It was frustrating, not understanding the way my body dealt with dysregulation.

I remember attending a high school sex ed class once but asking to be excused in the middle. It was graphic. I was processing. And the next thing I knew, I had bled through my t-shirt from picking my shoulder without even realizing it.

What I needed was a barrier between my skin and myself.

Now, when I'm in a situation that makes me uneasy, like commuting and arriving on time to events, I'll travel with a brace of some sort on. Depending where my picking spot is, I'll wear a finger, wrist, or elbow brace, which blocks any mindless attempt my fingers might make at bending and reaching my skin to pick.

This creates a barrier between me and my skin, preventing me from scanning then skin picking, while still getting where I need to go. And it works even better if you work this strategy into a particular environment that you pick in. Like putting the brace in the cup holder of your car, your coat, or your carry-on, for easy access in triggering travel scenarios.

Another difficult environment for my skin picking was any mirror in public places. I was already embarrassed by my actions with this illness, but I was even more horrified when I got stuck picking in public.

How many times did I get trapped in a dressing-room-mirror skin picking trance, only to come to from the fervent sound of knock, knock... at the door? All the times I heard "Are you okay in there?" still haunt me. No, I was not okay.

Now, I recommend that if you're visiting a new environment with a mirror, bring a pair of sunglasses to wear.

Inside.

Indoor sunglasses will allow you to still see what you need to but limit your vision (while adding mystique). With dimly lit vision, you won't be able to inspect your skin as precisely, preventing picking. Plus rock star level unlocked, IMO.

Lauren McKeaney

Week 4 Check-In

Have you been practicing mindfulness regularly?

- ☐ Yes, I practiced every single day this week.
- ☐ Yes, I practiced four to six times this week.
- ☐ Not quite, but I practiced one to three times this week.
- ☐ No, I did not practice this week.

How have you felt this week?

- ☐ Calm
- ☐ Anxious
- ☐ Bored
- ☐ Indifferent
- ☐ Relaxed
- ☐ Distracted
- ☐ Focused
- ☐ Sleepy
- ☐ Energized
- ☐ Other: ....

Have you noticed any of the following benefits in your life this week (even if just a little bit)?

- ☐ I'm more aware of when I'm doing my BFRB.

- ☐ I feel a little less anxious.
- ☐ I am not getting frustrated as often.
- ☐ I am more grateful for things that are going well.
- ☐ When I get upset, I can calm down more quickly.
- ☐ I'm sleeping better at night.
- ☐ I feel more rested during the day.
- ☐ I'm doing my BFRB a little bit less.
- ☐ When I notice I'm doing the BFRB, I can stop more quickly.
- ☐ Other: ....

How is your support system working?

- ☐ Great, no changes needed at all! I feel supported and held accountable by them.
- ☐ Pretty good, but it could be better.
- ☐ Okay, but it could use some changes.
- ☐ Not very good.
- ☐ What support system?

If you selected anything other than the first option, please go back to Chapter 6 and see what changes you can make to improve your support system. Below, write the steps that you will take right away to make sure that you get the support you need.

....

....

We will now cover the last two letters of SCAMP to help you identify and manage your motoric and environmental cues. Not sure what the heck I am talking about? Tune in below!

MOTORIC TRIGGERS

These are the specific motor movements (simply put, this is how we move our bodies) that lead up to and are involved in doing the behavior. Learning more about these movements will help you catch yourself as you start the movement before getting to the part where you do the damage. It will also help you come up with some tools to target those movements. Some examples of motoric triggers might be your arm moving up towards your head to get ready to pull or your fingers scanning your back, feeling for something to pick.

Drawing

Let's do an exercise together. Grab a pen or pencil and start by closing your eyes and picturing yourself doing your BFRB behavior. Now, draw a picture of yourself as you're doing the behavior. This could be a rough sketch or a beautiful piece of art—either is fine. No judgment here! Let's just get drawing!

Describing

Now answer the following questions to make sure you have a detailed understanding of your motoric triggers.

Are you usually aware of doing the behavior before you start?

- ☐ Yes
- ☐ No

Are there times when you are not consciously aware that you are doing the behavior, such as finding blood or hair and not having any recollection of picking or pulling?

- ☐ Yes
- ☐ No

When you are aware of doing the behavior, what posture or position are you usually in? (E.g., standing, sitting upright, reclining, lying down, etc.)

....

....

Do you use your fingers to scan your head or body looking for something to pull or pick?

- ☐ Yes
- ☐ No

Which hand(s) do you use to do the behavior? What position is your arm in?

....

....

What do you do with the skin or hair after you've picked or pulled it?

....

....

Motoric Strategies

Keeping in mind the cues you just identified, choose strategies that you think will best address each of your cues. Put a check by any that you'd like to try.

Awareness training:

- ☐ Mindfulness.
- ☐ Self-monitoring (tracking).
- ☐ Set reminders on your phone or around your house.

Response prevention/barriers:

- ☐ Wear Band-Aids or medical tape on fingertips, rubber fingers (from office supply stores to sort papers), or gloves.
- ☐ Wear glasses, even fake ones, to create a barrier to your eyelashes and eyebrows.
- ☐ Keep your hair wet to make it harder to pull.
- ☐ Use an elbow brace, thumb brace, wrist weight, or a bracelet with bells on it.
- ☐ Put Vaseline on your eyelids, eyebrows, or hair to make it harder to pull and increase growth.
- ☐ Wear a sleep mask to cover your eyebrows and lashes.
- ☐ Get rid of your tweezers.
- ☐ Wear a hat, bandana, scarf, or wig.
- ☐ Get hair extensions, which can be less satisfying to pull than your real hair.
- ☐ Change your hairstyle to a style that makes it harder to pull or makes you more aware.
- ☐ Cut fingernails short, get press on nails, or get acrylic, dip, or gel nails to make it harder to pick or pull. The acrylic or dip powder makes your nails thicker and less sharp, which makes it harder to pick your skin.

Competing response training:

- ☐ **Habit Reversal Training (HRT)**: Choose a behavior that, when you're doing it, means it's impossible to also do your BFRB. For many, this is clenching their fists or sitting on their hands. This will be your competing response (CR). Pay attention to your body to notice when you feel an urge to pick or pull, and as soon as you do, do your CR instead and hold it for

30 seconds. Then do 30 seconds of slow, deep breathing, and continue alternating between 30 seconds of the CR and 30 seconds of breathing until the urge passes.

- ☐ Hold something with both hands like a book, do a craft, or bounce a basketball.
- ☐ Fidget with something to keep your hands busy.

Putting It All Together

Now list out your motoric triggers and at least one strategy for each one that you'd be willing to try.

My motoric triggers	My motoric strategies

ENVIRONMENTAL MEDITATION

To jump into the final step of SCAMP, visit www.jkp.com/catalogue/book/9781805018650 or scan the QR code here to listen to the meditation and begin to notice more about the place or environment where you tend to pick or pull.

Environmental Meditation Inquiry

What did you notice during this meditation?

....

....

How is this exercise different from how you normally pay attention to your environment?

....

....

What is the point of this? How do you think practicing this meditation will help you manage your BFRB?

....

....

Environmental Triggers

Which locations do you tend to pick or pull in your home? Which rooms are you usually in when you do it? Which other locations do you do it in? (E.g., car, school, work, lying in bed, etc.)

....

....

Which activities are you engaging in when you pick or pull? (E.g., watching TV, playing on your phone, doing homework, reading, etc.)

....

....

Do you use any tools to help you pick or pull? (E.g., mirrors, tweezers, arm on table or armrest of couch, etc.)

....

....

When you feel the urge to engage in the behavior, is there anywhere you go or anything you do before starting the behavior?

....

....

Place/Environmental Strategies

Check any of the below that you'd like to try.

- ☐ **Decrease environmental cues**: Dim the lights in the bathroom, get rid of or cover mirrors, put a piece of paper up on your mirror covering the spot you lean in to to see your skin/hair, put makeup on in the kitchen using a small portable mirror, rearrange furniture, sit in a different place, avoid sitting where you can use an armrest.

- ☐ **Decrease privacy**: Leave doors open, go to bed when the rest of your family goes to bed, study/read/scroll your phone in a public area.
- ☐ Use a timer to decrease time spent in trigger areas and avoid doing the behavior without realizing when getting ready for school/work, after the shower, before bed, using the toilet.
- ☐ Avoid using screens late at night, because the light emitted makes it difficult to wind down.
- ☐ Have fidget toys or something to keep your hands busy while on your phone or computer. Leave these items somewhere you can easily grab them so that you will be sure to pick them up before you start scrolling.
- ☐ **Reminders**: Put Post-it notes in areas that you tend to pick or pull to remind you of strategies to use in that area or motivate you with inspirational quotes. Put up pictures of how you want your hair or skin to look on your mirror or in your car to help you stay motivated.
- ☐ Try to do mental tasks earlier in the day when you're more alert and physical tasks in the afternoon when people tend to feel more restless and are more likely to pick or pull.
- ☐ Wear gloves, Band-Aids, or tape on your fingers in high trigger areas like the car, bathroom, or bed.
- ☐ Have a variety of six or seven SCAMP objects/supplies in baskets or boxes within arm's length of every place your BFRB is a problem for you.

My Environmental Plan

Environmental triggers	Environmental strategies

REWARD PLAN

1. Choose up to three current (or past) strategies that are "working" to continue focusing on with this week's reward plan.
2. Add up to five new strategies to use in your plan.
3. Remember that you will be continually evaluating and adjusting these strategies to update your plan each week, so if you are torn between which to focus on this week, just choose up to five and go with it. There are no right or wrong strategies to pick.

MY REWARD PLAN

If I use . . . . strategies per . . . . (day or week) then I will earn: . . . .

Strategy	Mon	Tue	Wed	Thu	Fri	Sat	Sun

WEEK 5 ACTION STEPS

1. Practice mindfulness daily.
2. Choose up to five motoric, environmental, and/or other strategies to practice this week and write them on your reward chart above.
3. Connect with your support team and let them know your goals for the week.
4. Give yourself a sticker or smiley face on the chart whenever you practice mindfulness or one of your strategies.
5. When you earn a reward, cash it in! It's important to give yourself the reward and enjoy it so that it will continue to work as a reinforcer for your hard work.

- CHAPTER 12 -

Week 6: Sitting with the Urge

URGENT DELAYS

My BFRB urges webbed all over the place. And navigating my responses to them felt out of reach.

But I strengthened my ability to become aware of my skin picking urges, which made room for the next step.

Okay, you notice an urge, now what?

Well, once you recognize the urge, you can implement a way to delay it. And sometimes delaying it leads to no engagement at all. Imagine that.

Urge rerouting allows you to notice, delay, and reroute the urge. It's a way to shake things up from the norm of engaging in the picking.

For instance, if I noticed I was triggered while waiting in line, one hand scanning my chest for scabs to pick, I shifted my weight. This changed things. My balance was different. My hand moved, and I lost my grip on the scab. Then I saw something that distracted me. And the next thing I knew it was my turn to check out, so I started to pay. Skin picking prevented.

Often when I become aware I'm scanning, I'll first celebrate my awareness by saying out loud, "Woohoo!" This feel-good action reinforces me doing it again. And then I'll urge reroute and adjust my body posture. Lap around a table. Or my fav, go wash my hands.

Interrupting my BFRB with a new direction, like going to wash my hands, challenges the routine in my skin picking. It's also an everyday task that we are encouraged to perform throughout the day regardless and doesn't draw extra attention.

Plus, it keeps your hands super clean. Clean fingers reduce the spread of bacteria when you are picking on autopilot. And less bacteria means fewer skin irregularities that could tempt further exploration.

Lauren McKeaney

Week 5 Check-In

Have you been practicing mindfulness regularly?

- ☐ Yes, I practiced every single day this week.
- ☐ Yes, I practiced four to six times this week.
- ☐ Not quite, but I practiced one to three times this week.
- ☐ No, I did not practice this week.

How have you felt this week?

- ☐ Calm
- ☐ Anxious
- ☐ Bored
- ☐ Indifferent
- ☐ Relaxed
- ☐ Distracted
- ☐ Focused
- ☐ Sleepy
- ☐ Energized
- ☐ Other: ....

Have you noticed any of the following benefits in your life this week (even if just a little bit)?

- ☐ I'm more aware of when I'm doing my BFRB.
- ☐ I feel a little less anxious.
- ☐ I am not getting frustrated as often.
- ☐ I am more grateful for things that are going well.
- ☐ When I get upset, I can calm down more quickly.
- ☐ I'm sleeping better at night.
- ☐ I feel more rested during the day.
- ☐ I'm doing my BFRB a little bit less.
- ☐ When I notice I'm doing the BFRB, I can stop more quickly.
- ☐ Other: ....

How is your support system working?

- ☐ Great, no changes needed at all! I feel supported and held accountable by them.
- ☐ Pretty good, but it could be better.
- ☐ Okay, but it could use some changes.
- ☐ Not very good.
- ☐ What support system?

If you selected anything other than the first option, please go back to Chapter 6 and see what changes you can make to improve your support system. Below, write the steps that you will take right away to make sure that you get the support you need.

....

....

SITTING WITH AN URGE

This chapter will teach you a new way to respond to your urges.

> An urge is a strong, often sudden desire or compulsion to act in a specific way or engage in a particular behavior. It is an internal experience that can feel pressing or difficult to resist, and it often arises in response to certain thoughts, emotions, or external triggers.

Sitting with an urge is also called urge surfing. If you want to swim in the ocean, you have two choices. If you try to fight the waves or swim through them, you will likely get knocked down continually. However, if you ride the wave like you would on a surfboard, you can peacefully soar through the ocean.

When it comes to urge surfing, you don't even have to know how to surf in the ocean. This type of urge surfing doesn't involve any special skills or abilities. It just involves sitting still and letting yourself feel the urge. You feel the rise and fall of the urge and just let yourself ride the wave.

Choosing a New Path

As soon as you notice an urge to engage in the BFRB: Stop! You have come to a fork in the road and now you have two choices. One way has already been paved by your brain picking it over and over and over. It's the default path that gets chosen without any thought. It's the path towards doing the behavior, which could involve finding a good place to pick or just doing the behavior right then.

The second path, with only a few faint footprints, is the one that is very rarely taken. This path leads towards recovery, and it involves sitting with an urge without acting on it. It involves feeling the pain and discomfort and breathing along with it, remembering that this feeling won't last forever, and it's the only way to get on the other side of all of the urges.

How to Sit with an Urge

Below are some tips to help you gain success with this. This is a great time to remember that it is okay to be uncomfortable. That doesn't mean you are unsafe. You **can** be stronger than the urge!

Check each one you think would be helpful for you to remember.

- ☐ Sitting with an urge does not mean that we like it or that we want it around. It just means that we allow it to be as it is, and by **not** acting on it, we gradually learn that we can handle it.
- ☐ This may be **very** difficult, and feel almost impossible at first, so it must be done **very** gradually, starting with just a few seconds.
- ☐ You can do it as a formal mindfulness practice by doing the meditation or informally by not acting on the urge for a few minutes the next time you feel it.

Informal Practice

1. Find a spot on your skin or a hair that has been triggering you lately. Or if there isn't one currently, think of one that bothered you in the past.
2. Observe and describe in your mind what you notice using your senses. What exactly do you see or feel on your body?
3. Notice if any thoughts, emotions, or physical sensations come up for you as you're focusing on this. See if you can be aware of them and just allow them to be as they are for a few moments.
4. Notice any judgment, like "It feels bad," and try to describe it like you did the raisin in the mindful eating exercise in Week 1, using nonjudgmental language.

5. Try not to do the behavior even if you feel a strong urge to do it. See what it feels like to sit with the trigger and urge and not act on it.
6. If you cannot resist the urge and have to do the behavior, see if you can pick or pull mindfully. Do it in slow motion, noticing each movement and sensation like you did with mindful eating or mindfully brushing your teeth.
7. Check in with yourself. How do you feel now?

Formal Practice: Sitting with an Urge Meditation

Visit www.jkp.com/catalogue/book/9781805018650 or scan the QR code here.

Sitting with an Urge Meditation Inquiry

What did you observe during this meditation?

....

....

Did you notice any judgment coming up about the urge, the behavior, or yourself? If so, what did you do when you noticed the judgment?

....

....

How is this different from how you normally respond to the urge?

....

....

Do you think this meditation will help you manage your BFRB if you keep practicing it? If so, how? If not, why not?

....

....

Gradually Increasing Time Sitting with an Urge

- The next time that you have an urge to do the behavior, try to see if you can sit with the urge without doing the behavior for a few seconds. Even just counting to five and then engaging in the behavior is a good start to delaying the behavior.

- Even if you still pick or pull just as much, you are beginning to learn that you do not have to do the behavior every time that you have an urge.
- Once you are able to delay pretty consistently for a few seconds, try increasing the time very gradually. If five seconds is easy, try 10. If 30 seconds is easy, try one minute. Start with where you are comfortable and go just a little bit outside of your comfort zone.

SLOW AND STEADY WINS THE RACE

- To be successful with this, you must go slowly.
- If you go too quickly, it will be too difficult and you will get discouraged and give up.
- You want to stretch a little but still be successful.
- You want to feel some discomfort and learn that you can handle it and sit through it, so don't go too fast to the point where you can't handle it.
- If you think of your level of anxiety or discomfort on a scale of 1–10, with 1 being very comfortable and 10 being very uncomfortable, a level of 4–7 is a good level to strive for when sitting with urges.

Log Each Time You Sit with an Urge

- Use the chart below to keep track of what the urge feels like, if you did the behavior, how long you sat with it, how high your level of discomfort went, how low it went (if it went down while you were sitting with it), and what you learned from this.
- It is important to do this so that you can see if you are able to sit with the urge for longer periods over time and whether your discomfort level decreases the more you do it.
- This will likely be a very slow process, and consistency is more important than seeing changes right away.

Sitting with Urges Chart

Date/time	Describe the urge: What sensations, emotions, or thoughts did you notice? Did it change over time?	How long did you sit with it?	Did you do the behavior at all while sitting?	How high did the discomfort level go (1–10)?	How low did the discomfort level get (1–10)?	What did you learn?

HOW IS YOUR PLAN WORKING?

Think about the strategies you chose to use. Have you been using them somewhat often or regularly?

....

....

If not, what has gotten in the way and how can you work around these obstacles? (E.g., setting reminders on your phone, putting items needed in a more visible location.)

....

....

If so, how effective have they been in reducing your BFRB?

....

....

Are there any ways that you can adjust the strategies to make them more effective? (E.g., try them at different times of day, use them more often.)

....

....

Did you earn your reward this week? If so, did you give yourself the reward? If not, why not?

....

....

Adjusting Your Plan

Continue using any strategy that is working at least some of the time. Which strategies will you continue using?

....

....

Adjust those that need to be adjusted, and set up ways to overcome obstacles to using the strategies.

....

....

For every strategy that is not working and cannot be adjusted, choose a different strategy to use instead.

....

....

If all of your strategies are working, you may choose to add one additional strategy or just continue using the ones you've been using.

....

....

If your reward was not motivating enough, think of a different one that will really motivate you this week.

....

....

This will be a continual trial-and-error process, involving lots of evaluation and adjusting over time. The important thing is to not give up when things aren't working but instead just try something new!

....

....

MY NEW REWARD PLAN

If I use . . . . strategies per . . . . (day or week) then I will earn: . . . .

Strategy	Mon	Tue	Wed	Thu	Fri	Sat	Sun

WEEK 6 ACTION STEPS

1. Daily mindfulness practice. Choose what and when: . . . .
2. Practice sitting with the urge a few times a day.
3. Choose one to three other strategies to continue or start using this week.
4. Come up with a reward for using the strategies.
5. Let your support team know what you're working on this week and how they can help you. Tell your support team what the rewards are so that they can help you work towards them and reward you when you've earned them.

- CHAPTER 13 -

Week 7: Self-Compassion

LOVING SELF-LOVE

Once, I had an intense face picking flare-up right before a special dinner date with my mom. I was incredibly upset. I felt ashamed that it had happened yet again, and thought that I looked disgusting and everyone would be judging me. Plus, I didn't want to upset my mom and cancel. Again. I wasn't sure what to do.

Then, I reminded myself mistakes happen. Deep down, I knew the state of my skin made me uncomfortable, and acknowledging that took some of its power away. And when I asked myself what I really needed in that moment, the answer was clear: Staying in. Letting myself (and my skin) breathe. Even if that meant canceling plans with someone I wanted to be with.

Calling my mom to admit this was nerve-wracking. I thought I would feel like a failure. Especially since I wasn't going to make up a random excuse for canceling, like I usually would.

I took a deep breath and told her the truth. I was having a skin picking flare-up, but I had my strategies in place to manage it. I assured her she didn't need to worry and suggested rescheduling for another night.

In that moment, something surprising happened: I felt empowered.

I wasn't thrilled about the picking, of course. But I was proud that I had shown up for myself. And my mom? She responded with nothing but love and support, recognizing that I was making a healthy decision and taking care of myself.

Canceling dinner wasn't a failure. It was an act of self-love. And I loved it.

I was doing what I needed to do for me and my skin and putting my own compassionate care first. And recognizing how good it felt to feel good about something regarding my BFRB was intoxicating (and I wanted more).

Lauren McKeaney

Week 6 Check-In

Have you been practicing mindfulness regularly?

- ☐ Yes, I practiced every single day this week.
- ☐ Yes, I practiced four to six times this week.
- ☐ Not quite, but I practiced one to three times this week.
- ☐ No, I did not practice this week.

How have you felt this week?

- ☐ Calm
- ☐ Anxious
- ☐ Bored
- ☐ Indifferent
- ☐ Relaxed
- ☐ Distracted
- ☐ Focused
- ☐ Sleepy
- ☐ Energized
- ☐ Other: ....

Have you noticed any of the following benefits in your life this week (even if just a little bit)?

- ☐ I'm more aware of when I'm doing my BFRB.
- ☐ I feel a little less anxious.
- ☐ I am not getting frustrated as often.
- ☐ I am more grateful for things that are going well.
- ☐ When I get upset, I can calm down more quickly.
- ☐ I'm sleeping better at night.
- ☐ I feel more rested during the day.
- ☐ I'm doing my BFRB a little bit less.
- ☐ When I notice I'm doing the BFRB, I can stop more quickly.
- ☐ Other: ....

How is your support system working?

- ☐ Great, no changes needed at all! I feel supported and held accountable by them.
- ☐ Pretty good, but it could be better.
- ☐ Okay, but it could use some changes.
- ☐ Not very good.
- ☐ What support system?

If you selected anything other than the first option, please go back to Chapter 6 and see what changes you can make to improve your support system. Below, write the steps that you will take right away to make sure that you get the support you need.

....

....

WHAT IS SELF-COMPASSION?

Dr Kristin Neff defines self-compassion as treating yourself the way you treat a good friend. It involves three elements:

1. **Self-kindness**: Being understanding about things you don't like about yourself or mistakes you make.
2. **Common humanity**: Recognizing that making mistakes is part of being human, so you are not alone in feeling this way.
3. **Mindfulness**: Observing your negative thoughts and emotions with curiosity and openness while not over-identifying with them.

HOW WILL SELF-COMPASSION HELP ME?

Most people with BFRBs are very hard on themselves. Their self-judgments and criticisms are usually very harsh. You are probably much harder on yourself than you are on others. These judgments and criticisms usually make you feel horrible about yourself, which likely makes you do the behavior more. If you feel like you're a failure or ugly, why would you even try to stop the behavior? So much of your suffering is caused by your own self-judgment, which leads to more of the behavior and then more suffering, and the cycle of suffering seems endless.

What if, on the other hand, you could be kind and loving towards yourself? How do you think you'd feel if you could forgive yourself for what you've done to your skin or hair? Self-compassion can give you the support, empathy, and understanding that you get from good friends who are really there for you and make you feel good about yourself. If you can give this to yourself, you will be able to access these good feelings anytime. When you are feeling better, you are likely to do the behavior less, which will make you feel even better, putting into effect a cycle of healthy behaviors, thoughts, and feelings.

Self-Compassion Meditation

Visit www.jkp.com/catalogue/book/9781805018650 or scan the QR code here.

Self-Compassion Meditation Inquiry

What did you notice during this meditation?

How is this different from how you normally talk to yourself?

How could this be helpful for you in dealing with your BFRB?

Exploring Self-Compassion through Writing

This exercise is one of Dr Kristin Neff's writing exercises on her website, https://self-compassion.org.

Part 1: Which imperfections make you feel not good enough?

Everybody has something about themselves that they don't like—something that causes them to feel shame, insecure, or not "good enough." Try writing about how your BFRB makes you feel bad about yourself (like with physical appearance, at school/work, or in your relationships). What emotions come up for you when you think about this? Try to just feel your emotions without trying to change them or push them away, and then write about them.

....

....

....

....

....

....

....

....

....

Part 2: Write a letter to yourself from the perspective of an unconditionally loving imaginary friend

Now think about an imaginary friend who is unconditionally loving, accepting, kind, and compassionate. Imagine that this friend can see all your strengths and all your challenges, including the aspects of yourself you have just been writing about. Reflect upon what this friend feels towards you and how you are loved and accepted exactly as you are, with all of your very human imperfections and quirks. This friend recognizes the limits of human nature and is kind and forgiving towards you. In his/her great wisdom, this friend understands your life history and the millions of things that have happened in your life to create you as you are in this moment. Your BFRB is connected to so many things you didn't necessarily choose: your genes, your family history, life circumstances—things that were outside of your control.

Write a letter to yourself from the perspective of this imaginary friend—focusing on the parts of your BFRB that you tend to judge yourself for. What would this friend say to you about your "flaw" from the perspective of someone who truly appreciates you and wants the best for you? How would this friend convey their empathy for you, especially for the pain you feel when you judge yourself so harshly? What would this friend write in order to remind you that you are only human, that all people have both strengths and weaknesses? And if you think this friend would suggest possible changes you should make, how would these suggestions be conveyed lovingly to you? As you write to yourself from the perspective of this imaginary friend, try to infuse your letter with a strong sense of his/her acceptance, kindness, care, and desire for your health and happiness.

Part 3: Feel the compassion as it soothes and comforts you

After writing the letter, put it down for a little while. Then come back and read it again, really letting the words sink in. Feel the compassion as you review what you wrote. Let yourself be reminded that people care about you and of the importance of caring about yourself. Showing yourself compassion and kindness starts on the inside and works its way out.

Kindness in Action

Take a few moments to bring to mind what you do during a typical week. Jot down 10 of the activities that make up your life at home, school, or work.

1. ....

2. ....

3. ....

4. ....

5. ....

6. ....

7. ....

8. ....

9. ....

10. ....

Now go back and place a + next to the activities that lift your mood, are energizing, or make you feel good in some way. Then place a – next to ones that are draining, depleting, or make you feel bad in some way.

What do you notice about the effect the activities you do have on your mood?

....

....

....

Did anything surprise you about this exercise?

....

....

....

What you do affects how you feel. Most importantly, you can change how you feel by changing what you do. You can turn activity into a simple, yet powerful way to raise your mood and enhance your well-being.

Activities that Help: Pleasure and Mastery

When people feel down, exhausted, and lacking energy, there are two types of activities that are particularly effective ways to lift their mood:

- **Pleasure activities**: Things that give you a sense of enjoyment, like calling a friend, taking a walk, listening to music, or watching a good movie.
- **Mastery activities**: Things that give you a sense of accomplishment, like doing your homework, cleaning, or doing something you've been putting off.

My list of pleasure activities

Make a list of activities that you enjoy doing.

1. ....
2. ....
3. ....
4. ....
5. ....
6. ....
7. ....
8. ....
9. ....
10. ....

My list of mastery activities

Write a list of activities that make you feel good after completing them.

1. ....
2. ....
3. ....
4. ....
5. ....
6. ....

7. ....

8. ....

9. ....

10. ....

Don't forget that **intention** is key. The same behaviors can have very different results depending on your intention. If you do an activity to try to get rid of a "bad" feeling, urge, or behavior, it will likely backfire and make you feel worse when you don't feel better right away. Instead, do the activity to be kind to yourself—as a little treat that you give yourself. You will likely find that this shift in intention will result in a greater likelihood that the desired shift in mood will occur or at least start to head in that direction. Often when you're really struggling, it takes time to feel better, and one activity is not going to shift your mood much, but over time, this continued self-care will have a positive impact on your mood.

WEEK 7 ACTION STEPS

1. Do the self-compassion meditation daily as your formal practice, and try some activities of pleasure or mastery as informal mindfulness practices.
2. Think about what you need most right now. Do you need a break from the strategies you've been using, or are they helping and you'd like to continue them? Are you feeling overwhelmed with so much to do and track? If so, just do the first action step on here and give yourself the break you need this week.
3. If you want to continue using strategies, choose the ones you'd like to use and set a new reward plan.
4. Check in with your support team to let them know what your goals are for the week and how and when they can check in on you for support and accountability.

MY NEW REWARD PLAN

If I use . . . . strategies per . . . . (day or week) then I will earn: . . . .

Strategy	Mon	Tue	Wed	Thu	Fri	Sat	Sun

- CHAPTER 14 -

Week 8: Resume Doing What You Love

FREE TO BE ME

My relationship with showing skin was complicated.

I'd watch classmates effortlessly switch from hoodies to t-shirts, pulling them over their heads (showing arm skin!) without a second thought. In gym class, friends sported shorts like it was nothing, while I sweated in my sweats, covered up from top to toe. I'd lie about being on my period to get out of swimming, from thinking my body had too many sores and scars to be seen.

Jealousy and judgment consumed me.

I longed for the freedom to wear what I wanted instead of what hid my wounds. But at the time, it felt easier to stay covered than to answer questions I didn't yet know how to answer about my skin and skin picking.

Senior year, I had a constellation of arm and shoulder sores that wouldn't heal for months. I also had a stunning mint green and gold spaghetti-strap dress I dreamed of wearing to prom. But I knew I didn't feel comfortable wearing it, yet.

So I decided to start small.

After spring break, I rolled up my sleeves in school. It was barely noticeable to anyone else, but to me, it was everything. That small step made it easier to transition to t-shirts next. Short sleeves went well, but tank tops took a little more time, as they exposed upper arm scars from my BFRB.

When it came time for prom, I surprised myself and slipped right into the dress. I felt beautiful and fun and carefree. I loved it! I was proud of myself and my achievement, and I attribute successfully wearing that stunner to my gradual approach of showing more and more skin (mini goals, mega wins).

And this has followed me to this day. At the Picking Me Foundation, we like to say that you don't have to worry about being ready if you work on becoming ready.

Lauren McKeaney

Week 7 Check-In

Have you been practicing mindfulness regularly?

- ☐ Yes, I practiced every single day this week.
- ☐ Yes, I practiced four to six times this week.
- ☐ Not quite, but I practiced one to three times this week.
- ☐ No, I did not practice this week.

How have you felt this week?

- ☐ Calm
- ☐ Anxious
- ☐ Bored
- ☐ Indifferent
- ☐ Relaxed
- ☐ Distracted
- ☐ Focused
- ☐ Sleepy
- ☐ Energized
- ☐ Other: ....

Have you noticed any of the following benefits in your life this week (even if just a little bit)?

- ☐ I'm more aware of when I'm doing my BFRB.
- ☐ I feel a little less anxious.
- ☐ I am not getting frustrated as often.
- ☐ I am more grateful for things that are going well.
- ☐ When I get upset, I can calm down more quickly.
- ☐ I'm sleeping better at night.
- ☐ I feel more rested during the day.
- ☐ I'm doing my BFRB a little bit less.
- ☐ When I notice I'm doing the BFRB, I can stop more quickly.
- ☐ Other: ....

How is your support system working?

- ☐ Great, no changes needed at all! I feel supported and held accountable by them.
- ☐ Pretty good, but it could be better.
- ☐ Okay, but it could use some changes.
- ☐ Not very good.
- ☐ What support system?

If you selected anything other than the first option, please go back to Chapter 6 and see what changes you can make to improve your support system. Below, write the steps that you will take right away to make sure that you get the support you need.

....

....

ARE YOU AVOIDING THINGS YOU WANT TO DO?

Since it's unlikely that you will ever completely stop doing the BFRB, in order to lead a full, happy life, you will need to push yourself to get back to doing some of the things that you've been avoiding. It's normal to avoid things that make us uncomfortable, and if they're things that you don't care about, like spiders, then it's okay to keep avoiding them. However, when it comes to something that you do like, such as swimming, or something that means you will be left out of an activity with friends if you don't do it and you value your friendships, then learning to face your fears is going to be important.

ANXIETY CYCLE

To understand how avoidance reinforces your anxiety, it helps to plug your specific triggers, thoughts, emotions, and avoidant coping mechanisms into the anxiety cycle. This cycle also works for most unwanted emotional states, like depression or anger, and could also be used to conceptualize the cycle of your BFRB.

For the purpose of this exercise, list any situations, people, places, or things that make you anxious because of your BFRB. Then write out some of your anxious thoughts about these triggers. For instance, if you listed swimming as a trigger, then write your thoughts about what will happen if you swim or why you're anxious about it, such as, "If I swim, my makeup will come off and everyone will judge me for having so many spots that I've picked."

Then identify the emotions that you experience when you are faced with these triggers. Finally, identify the things that you do to avoid feeling these emotions. These include both the people, places, things, and situations that you actually avoid, like swimming pools and wearing swimsuits, and the other more subtle ways to avoid the emotions. Internal processes like worrying, ruminating, distracting yourself, and overthinking are some of these more subtle forms of avoidance. Some of these may seem like they are not avoidance because they involve giving a lot of attention to the subject matter, but they are still avoidance because they are usually done in an effort to reduce or get rid of the unpleasant emotions.

The short-term outcome of avoidant coping is usually some relief of anxiety or other unwanted emotions, but this usually only lasts for a short time. The long-term outcome of avoidance tends to be increased anxiety. Using the example of swimming again, if you avoid swimming, then your distorted beliefs get reinforced because you never learn that the feared outcomes of everyone judging you negatively may not occur, or that even if they do occur, you can handle them. Therefore, this cycle shows us how our avoidance is actually what fuels our anxiety. Every time you avoid something that you are afraid of, your fear grows stronger.

Sample Anxiety Cycle

What is the situation that made you uncomfortable?

Swimming, wearing swimsuit without a cover-up, going to swimming party, wearing tank tops.

What are your false beliefs about this?

If I swim, all my makeup will come off and everyone will judge my skin. I can't let anyone know that I pick my skin because they'd never understand. No one will invite me to these parties anymore once they see how my skin really looks.

How do these beliefs make you feel?

Anxious, embarrassed, frustrated, scared, angry, sad, disappointed.

What are you avoiding because of your false beliefs?

Don't go swimming, avoid swimming parties, keep swimsuit covered if have to be at swimming event, stay outside of the pool, wear long-sleeve shirts no matter how hot it is.

How do you feel after you avoid the situation (usually a temporary relief of anxiety)?

I feel relieved at first that I don't have to go, but then feel sad that I'm missing out again.

What is the long-term impact of your avoidance?

Makes distorted beliefs feel more true, makes anxiety stronger, and never learn that I can handle facing my fears.

My Anxiety Cycle

Now it's your turn to fill this out using your own triggers, distorted beliefs, emotional responses, and avoidant coping responses.

What is the situation that made you uncomfortable?

....

What are your false beliefs about this?

....

How do these beliefs make you feel?

....

What are you avoiding because of your false beliefs?

....

How do you feel after you avoid the situation?

....

What is the long-term impact of your avoidance?

....

HEALTHY COPING CYCLE

Healthy coping involves finding ways to manage your anxiety without avoidance so that you can gradually face your fears without an overload of anxiety.

Identifying Healthy Beliefs

As we talked about in Chapter 10 (Week 4: Thinking and Feeling Strategies) on thoughts, you can't stop the unhealthy thoughts but you can create healthier ones to replace them. For instance, for the belief about swimming, you could say something like, "It's likely that no one will judge me, and even if they do, I can handle it." Write beliefs that are balanced and believable so that when you read them to yourself, you will feel like you're stretching a little but still believe it. If you say something like, "Everyone will think I look awesome," then you won't believe this and it won't help. For any distorted beliefs that you have trouble coming up with a healthy belief for, you can use the thought challenging worksheet to help (you'll find a blank version at the end of this chapter).

Identifying Healthy Behaviors

Next, think about things that you can do to help yourself relax or reduce your anxiety, such as taking deep breaths, going for a walk, talking to a friend, taking a bath, or meditating. In addition to things that you'll do to manage your anxiety, the other important healthy coping behavior is gradually facing your fears. This is actually the key to breaking free from your anxiety. Once you do the things you've been afraid to do, then anxiety won't be able to hold you back anymore.

Outcomes of Healthy Coping

The outcomes of healthy coping are essentially the opposites of the outcomes of the anxiety cycle. When you face your fears, you will likely feel more anxious at first as you are doing things that you've avoided in the past. However, as you continue to face your fears, it will get easier over time, and you will learn that you are able to handle the feared situations and the resulting anxiety. So the long-term outcomes include not only expanding the circle of activities you engage in but also reducing your anxiety in all situations, including new ones.

Healthy Cycle

Fill in this cycle with healthy beliefs that you could use to challenge your distorted beliefs. Then write in some things you could do to help manage your anxiety and some steps you could take to start facing your fears.

Healthy beliefs

....

Healthy behaviors

....

Short-term outcome of healthy coping

I may experience an increase in anxiety, especially when I gradually face my fears.

....

....

Long-term outcome of healthy coping

I'll learn that I can handle facing my fears and that the feared outcomes do not occur or are not as difficult to handle as I thought they'd be.

....

....

CREATING A HIERARCHY

Before you face your fears, you need to create a hierarchy of feared situations, people, places, and things. To do this, make a list of all the things that you avoid, and then rate how high your anxiety level would be on a scale of 1–10 if you were to face this fear. Then place these items on the hierarchy, listing them in order from least to most anxiety provoking. If all of your items are in the medium to high level of anxiety, see if you can break any of these items into parts to make them easier to face. For instance, if going to a pool party with friends is a 9, think about what level your anxiety would be to go swimming with just one friend or family member and add that to the hierarchy. You can also think about what your anxiety level would be to go to a pool party wearing your regular clothes and not getting in the water.

My Feared Situations, People, Places, and Things

1. ....

2. ....

3. ....

4. ....

5. ....

6. ....

7. ....

Feared Task Hierarchy

Next, put each item above into one of these three categories, depending on how high your anxiety would be to do that thing.

Low level exposures (anxiety level 1–3)

....

....

Medium level exposures (anxiety level 4–6)

....

....

High level exposures (anxiety level 7–10)

....

....

GRADUAL EXPOSURE

The key to facing your fears is to do it **gradually**. Start by choosing an item on your hierarchy that is in the low or medium level that you'd like to try to do. It's best to start small, so choose something that will cause the lowest level of anxiety possible. Before you do the exposure, start filling out the first five columns on your exposure log to indicate the day, time, what the exposure is, what your fears predict will happen, and what your pre-exposure anxiety level is. If you are feeling anxious or worried about doing the exposure, you can use the thought challenging sheet to challenge any distorted thoughts and come up with a healthier thought that will help you face your fear.

Exposure Log

Date	Time	Exposure (What are you going to do to face a fear?)	What does your fear predict will happen?	Pre-exposure anxiety level (1–10)	Highest level of anxiety during the exposure	How low did your anxiety get while doing the exposure?	What actually happened? What did you learn from doing this?

Then go ahead and do your first exposure. You can continue to remind yourself of your healthy beliefs that you've created as needed during the exposure, but it is important to let yourself sit with the anxiety rather than do things to try to make it go away completely. Similar to how you learned to sit with an urge, sitting with anxiety gets easier over time if you practice regularly. The more consistently you practice, the more quickly your anxiety levels will go down. Log each completed exposure, making sure to reflect on what you learned from doing this; for example, "I can handle sitting with some anxiety."

SITTING WITH DIFFICULTIES MEDITATION

This meditation is one of the best ways to practice sitting with your anxiety. It's similar to the sitting with an urge meditation, but it is for sitting with difficult emotions. Now is the perfect time to try this, since you've just been thinking about all of your triggers and how you will face your fears. Visit www.jkp.com/catalogue/book/9781805018650 or scan the QR code above.

Sitting with Difficulties Meditation Inquiry

What did you notice during this meditation?

How is this different from what you normally do when you're feeling something uncomfortable?

How could this help you face your fears?

WEEK 8 ACTION STEPS

1. Practice the sitting with difficulties meditation daily to keep up your formal mindfulness practice and practice sitting with anxiety.

2. Do daily (or as often as possible) exposure to feared situations, places, people, and things that you'd like to be able to face.
3. Log each exposure and use the thought challenging and/or any other healthy coping strategies to help manage your anxiety.
4. Create a reward plan for this week.
5. Check in with your support team about how they can best support you this week.

MY NEW REWARD PLAN

If I use .... strategies per .... (day or week) then I will earn: ....

Strategy	Mon	Tue	Wed	Thu	Fri	Sat	Sun

THOUGHT CHALLENGING

What is the situation that is bothering you?

....

....

What thoughts are popping into your mind about it? What are you worried will happen?

....

....

Circle the "hot thought," the one that makes you feel the worst.

How true does this thought **feel** (0–100%)? ....

List the evidence that suggests that this thought is true.

....

....

List the evidence that suggests that this thought is **not** true or not completely true.

....

....

Identify the false beliefs or thinking errors that are making you believe that this thought is true.

....

....

Using logic and facts, how true do you think it actually is (0–100%)? ....

Develop a balanced belief, taking into account the work completed above.

....

....

- CHAPTER 15 -

Week 9: Am I in Recovery?

HAPPY HEALING

Recovery is different for everyone.

I think it's understanding that even if I pick, I still matter. My worth isn't valued by skin.

Recovery doesn't necessarily mean cured, and you don't have to be cured to live your life.

There is no cure for skin picking disorder. For me, I say I'm in recovery with, not from, it. With it because it's something I take on and manage daily. And doing so helps me live the full life I deserve to live.

That's recovery.

It's covering my mirrors. It's dimming my lights. It's telling friends. Short nails. Resilience. On repeat.

I used to think I had to be pick-free to be recovered from my BFRB. To me, any picking symbolized defeat.

How can I be considered to be healing while having actual wounds (sometimes wide) open on my body?

Then, one year, I was invited to speak on a Recovery Panel at a mental health conference. The night before, I had a flare-up in the hotel bathroom mirror (aren't those the worst?!), picking at a scab over my eyebrow. The next morning, running late for my live session, I fashioned a Band-Aid over the large sore above my eye and rushed to the conference.

As I sat on that stage with fellow panelists, I suddenly felt like I didn't belong. Could I really call myself "in recovery" with a huge Band-Aid on my face from a picking episode hours earlier?

The answer was, and still is, yes.

Showing up, staying committed to my goals, and sharing my story is recovery. Recovery isn't about never picking again. It's about not letting it define me. It's about choosing to live a life aligned with my values, despite the struggles. It's staying committed. And trying. Again.

It's ongoing and worth it.

Remember, the picking might not completely stop. But the suffering can.

Reach out and let me know your thoughts on skin picking recovery at lauren@pickingme.org.

Lauren McKeaney

Week 8 Check-In

Have you been practicing mindfulness regularly?

- ☐ Yes, I practiced every single day this week.
- ☐ Yes, I practiced four to six times this week.
- ☐ Not quite, but I practiced one to three times this week.
- ☐ No, I did not practice this week.

How have you felt this week?

- ☐ Calm
- ☐ Anxious
- ☐ Bored
- ☐ Indifferent
- ☐ Relaxed
- ☐ Distracted
- ☐ Focused
- ☐ Sleepy
- ☐ Energized
- ☐ Other: ....

Have you noticed any of the following benefits in your life this week (even if just a little bit)?

- ☐ I'm more aware of when I'm doing my BFRB.
- ☐ I feel a little less anxious.
- ☐ I am not getting frustrated as often.
- ☐ I am more grateful for things that are going well.
- ☐ When I get upset, I can calm down more quickly.
- ☐ I'm sleeping better at night.

- ☐ I feel more rested during the day.
- ☐ I'm doing my BFRB a little bit less.
- ☐ When I notice I'm doing the BFRB, I can stop more quickly.
- ☐ Other: ....

How is your support system working?

- ☐ Great, no changes needed at all! I feel supported and held accountable by them.
- ☐ Pretty good, but it could be better.
- ☐ Okay, but it could use some changes.
- ☐ Not very good.
- ☐ What support system?

If you selected anything other than the first option, please go back to Chapter 6 and see what changes you can make to improve your support system. Below, write the steps that you will take right away to make sure that you get the support you need.

....

....

WHAT DOES RECOVERY LOOK LIKE?

Completely stopping the behavior is often not realistic, and this perfectionistic view can be harmful. Humans are not perfect, so if you attempt to be perfectly recovered, you will be setting yourself up to be disappointed.

BFRBs are chronic and do not have a cure. Recovery with BFRBs usually means that the behavior is under control and the person can resume a normal, happy life. It is important to recognize the potential for the behavior to return, even when it does stop completely, so that you can be ready and prepared to deal with it.

REALISTIC VIEW OF RECOVERY

Your behavior is reduced to the point of only occurring occasionally. When you engage in the behavior, you are able to stop before it gets out of control, meaning you've only picked or pulled a little bit. There is no more new visible damage, so you are able to wear your hair however you want and wear whatever clothing you want without the worry of others noticing bald spots or open wounds. When you do have an occasional time when you start to go back to doing your BFRB again, you are able to continue to accept yourself and engage in your relapse prevention plan.

PICTURE YOUR LIFE IN RECOVERY MEDITATION

Visit www.jkp.com/catalogue/book/9781805018650 or scan the QR code here.

Picture Your Life in Recovery Meditation Inquiry

What did you notice during this meditation?

....

....

....

How is this picture of recovery different from your current life?

....

....

....

How could this meditation be helpful in your recovery?

....

....

....

What Your Recovery Looks Like

How will you know when you are in recovery?

....

....

....

What will be different in your life?

....

....

....

How will you view yourself differently?

....

....

....

What things will you be doing that you're not doing now?

....

....

What will you be doing to cope with your stress and difficulties that arise in your life besides engaging in your BFRB?

....

....

....

WEEK 9 ACTION STEPS

1. Make a plan for daily formal and informal mindfulness practice that is sustainable over time.
2. Plan which strategies you will continue to use and how you will know if they're working or not.
3. Create a reward plan for your weekly practice, thinking about how you will keep adjusting your reward plan over time to keep you motivated.
4. Check in with your support system about the plan for this week and start discussing how you'll keep up your progress after the 10-week program.

MY NEW REWARD PLAN

If I use . . . . strategies per . . . . (day or week) then I will earn: . . . .

Strategy	Mon	Tue	Wed	Thu	Fri	Sat	Sun

- CHAPTER 16 -

Week 10: Relapse Prevention

AGAIN ISN'T FOREVER

As this is a chronic condition, it's important to accept that relapses are likely, but not a life sentence.

And while we may not be able to control every aspect of our BFRB journey, we can control how we respond to it.

By accepting myself post-pick, acknowledging that it happened and that now's a new moment, I avoid spiraling into a sabotage cycle. By being gentle and not tearing myself apart further, I don't get derailed. Instead, I get ready to try again.

This kindness gives me space to learn from the episode. That active learning keeps the momentum going, helping me continue managing my recovery and working towards progress (rather than dwelling in defeat).

Building and working with your support system on your BFRB journey creates accountability and growth. For more relapse management, connection, and support, I highly recommend finding a support group for BFRBs.

Being part of a support group was and has been integral in my skin picking recovery. Especially during flare-ups. These meetings provide opportunities to validate experiences, listen and be heard, and stay engaged in the process. All with your people.

The Picking Me Foundation runs the largest and longest running online skin picking support group and has hosted over 5,500 attendees. It's an honor and a privilege to lead these meetings, and you can learn more at https://pickingme.org/onlinesupportgroup. I hope to see you there!

Here's to you and #PickingMe over skin picking.

You've got this, loves. Much love and support.

Lauren McKeaney

Week 9 Check-In

Have you been practicing mindfulness regularly?

- ☐ Yes, I practiced every single day this week.
- ☐ Yes, I practiced four to six times this week.
- ☐ Not quite, but I practiced one to three times this week.
- ☐ No, I did not practice this week.

How have you felt this week?

- ☐ Calm
- ☐ Anxious
- ☐ Bored
- ☐ Indifferent
- ☐ Relaxed
- ☐ Distracted
- ☐ Focused
- ☐ Sleepy
- ☐ Energized
- ☐ Other: ....

Have you noticed any of the following benefits in your life this week (even if just a little bit)?

- ☐ I'm more aware of when I'm doing my BFRB.
- ☐ I feel a little less anxious.
- ☐ I am not getting frustrated as often.
- ☐ I am more grateful for things that are going well.
- ☐ When I get upset, I can calm down more quickly.
- ☐ I'm sleeping better at night.
- ☐ I feel more rested during the day.
- ☐ I'm doing my BFRB a little bit less.
- ☐ When I notice I'm doing the BFRB, I can stop more quickly.
- ☐ Other: ....

How is your support system working?

- ☐ Great, no changes needed at all! I feel supported and held accountable by them.
- ☐ Pretty good, but it could be better.
- ☐ Okay, but it could use some changes.
- ☐ Not very good.
- ☐ What support system?

If you selected anything other than the first option, please go back to Chapter 6 and see what changes you can make to improve your support system. Below, write the steps that you will take right away to make sure that you get the support you need.

....

....

Now that you've officially finished this program, go back and complete the questionnaire in Chapter 2 again to see if your responses have changed. If they have changed in a positive direction (less BFRB symptoms), congratulations! If not, consider what might have caused this lack of change. Sometimes we find that people underestimate their symptoms, and once they learn more and pay more attention to the BFRB, they notice that things are actually worse than they thought. Another possibility is that you didn't devote enough time or effort to this book. If you feel this is true, you can consider whether you can give more time or effort and, if so, go back through the book and redo the material. If you are feeling hopeless and unsure of how to work through this, contact a mental health professional who specializes in BFRBs to help navigate this with you.

RELAPSE PREVENTION

Once you've reached recovery with your BFRB, you will need a relapse prevention plan to stay in recovery. Drs. G. Alan Marlatt and Judith R. Gordon, two researchers in alcohol abuse treatment, coined the term "relapse prevention" in 1985, referring to a series of four steps to stay in recovery.[1] We'll use those steps as our guide in creating your relapse prevention plan.

1 Marlatt, G. A. and Gordon, J. R. (eds) (1985) *Relapse Prevention: Maintenance Strategies in the Treatment of Addictive Behaviors.* New York: Guilford Press.

STEP 1: KNOW YOUR HOT SPOTS

You've already identified the situations, places, emotions, thoughts, and sensory needs that tend to trigger your behavior. Next, you'll identify the series of behaviors that you do before doing the behavior. You can think of this as a chain of behaviors that gets stronger with each subsequent link. Behavioral chains are easier to break if you interrupt them in their earlier stages. Write out a few typical behavioral chains for your common triggers, separating out each step to really break it down.

Sample Behavior Chain

1. Driving home from school feeling tired and stressed.
2. Walking into your house and putting your stuff down.
3. Walking into the kitchen and heating up some food.
4. Walking into your room and sitting down in your chair.
5. Getting on your phone with one hand, while the other starts to play with your hair.
6. Noticing a hair that feels thicker, you pull it out.
7. Feeling for other hairs to pull.
8. Continuing to pull until you realize that you're starving and you left your food in the microwave.

My Behavior Chain

Pick one of your common triggering situations and write out the steps that typically lead up to you picking or pulling.

1. ....
2. ....
3. ....
4. ....
5. ....
6. ....
7. ....
8. ....
9. ....
10. ....

How to Break the Chain

The sooner you recognize that this behavioral chain is occurring, the better your chances are of breaking it. For instance, when you recognize that you're tired and stressed on the way home, you could plan to do something that is less likely to end in pulling, like taking a shower or doing a craft that requires both hands. Or if you decide to sit and look on your phone, being aware of this typical chain can remind you to put on gloves, put your hair up, and/or not sit on that specific chair.

Waiting to intervene until your hand is already in your hair could be problematic, because at this point it will be much harder to stop yourself. Remembering your triggers and recognizing when these chains are starting are your cues to take action to prevent yourself from engaging in the behavior. Identify where you'll break each of your chains and write out what you'll do to break the chain.

How I'll Break the Chain

Go back and look at your behavioral chain and list an idea of how you could break the chain for each step.

1. ....
2. ....
3. ....
4. ....
5. ....
6. ....
7. ....
8. ....
9. ....
10. ....

Coping Statements

Preparing yourself verbally before going into a potentially triggering situation can also help to stop you doing the behavior. Here are some examples. Check any that you think would be helpful for you to use and then add some of your own.

- ☐ "This is the challenge I've been training for."
- ☐ "This will be uncomfortable, but I can do it."

- ☐ "Resist the urge and it will pass."
- ☐ "I don't like this, but I can stand it."
- ☐ "I can't choose whether or not I feel an urge or get tempted, but I can choose how to react to it."
- ☐ "If I want to be well, I have to resist it."
- ☐ "Okay, get ready, here it comes."
- ☐ ....
- ☐ ....
- ☐ ....
- ☐ ....
- ☐ ....
- ☐ ....

Imaginal Rehearsal

Another technique to use before going into a potentially triggering situation is to visualize yourself going through the situation and resisting the urge to act on the behavior. Start by closing your eyes and focusing on your breathing to get yourself into a calm state in the present moment. Then imagine yourself successfully using your strategies while you go through the situation without engaging in the behavior.

Imaginal Rehearsal Inquiry

What did you notice when doing this imaginal rehearsal?

....

....

How is this different from how you normally experience this situation?

....

....

How could this be helpful for you in managing your BFRB?

....

....

STEP 2: PREPARE FOR SETBACKS

Setbacks are a normal part of recovery, because no matter how well you've recovered, no one is perfect. In order to maintain your recovery, you need to prepare for these slips and not beat yourself up or get depressed or anxious when they occur. Remember that a setback is not a relapse, meaning that it does not take you back to where you were before you learned all of the strategies and did all of the hard work to get to recovery.

Just as acceptance of the behavior was an important part of your recovery, acceptance of setbacks will keep you in recovery. However, be careful not to allow this acceptance to alter your decision in the moment to continue the behavior (e.g., "It's okay to keep picking") or to tell yourself that since setbacks are inevitable, there's no point trying to resist. A setback can be viewed as a valuable learning experience if you learn from whatever mistakes led to it and then use it as an opportunity to practice using your skills to get back on track.

Coping with Setbacks

What tools that you've learned in this book will help you cope with a setback? Check all that you think would be helpful and add your own ideas.

- ☐ Do a body scan or other meditation to help regulate your emotions.
- ☐ Do an informal mindfulness practice like taking a walk or petting your dog or cat.
- ☐ Reach out to someone on your support team to let them know and ask for support.
- ☐ Resume tracking for one week to gain awareness and gather ideas for where to implement strategies.
- ☐ Choose two or three sensory strategies to use for one week.
- ☐ Choose two or three cognitive or affective strategies to use for one week.
- ☐ Choose two or three motoric or environmental strategies to use for one week.
- ☐ Create a reward plan to track your use of strategies.
- ☐ Use the sitting with an urge meditation or informal practice.
- ☐ Write a letter to yourself from the perspective of a loving friend.
- ☐ Listen to the self-compassion meditation.
- ☐ Do an activity of pleasure or mastery to help lift your mood.
- ☐ Plan exposures to get you back to doing more things that you love to do.

- ☐ ....
- ☐ ....
- ☐ ....

STEP 3: ACT IMMEDIATELY ON SETBACKS

The other key to handling setbacks is to recognize what is happening and get back on track ASAP, because the more time that passes, the harder it will be to do so and the more damage that will be done. To stay in recovery, you must recognize that **you** are responsible for how you manage your behavior, and this is especially true when it comes to handling setbacks. If you blame your behavior on the illness or someone or something that triggered you, then you will have much less success in managing your behavior.

Now that you have learned strategies that are successful for you, you always have a choice to use one instead of doing the behavior, no matter how difficult this is. You are now your own coach, so you need to determine what you need to do and do it. Remember that you can always start over, so if you pick or pull some, don't give up for the rest of the day. The sooner you get back to using your strategies, the better.

Common Misunderstood Facts/Thoughts about Setbacks

Recognizing cognitive distortions and talking back to the thoughts is a crucial tool in providing yourself with the support you need during this difficult time. What you tell yourself will often be the determining factor between a setback turning into a relapse or you staying in recovery.

Check the thoughts that you can relate to. Then below each one, write a healthier thought that you could say to yourself instead.

- ☐ **Overgeneralizing**: Telling yourself that one setback indicates that a total relapse is occurring and that it's a sign of complete failure on your part. For example, "Since I messed up this time, I will always continue to mess up and will never really be better."

Healthier thought: ....

- ☐ **Selective filter**: Selecting a particular negative event or detail and focusing on it alone and ignoring your previous hard work and achievements. For example, "All of my hard work was a waste because I just pulled out all of the hair that had grown back."

Healthier thought: ....

- ☐ **All-or-nothing thinking**: You see yourself as a total success or complete failure. For example, "I'm a failure because I've messed up."

Healthier thought: ....

☐ **Catastrophizing**: You think of a setback as the worst possible thing that could have happened to you and think that it will lead to other horrible consequences. "Now that I'm pulling again, I'll never have a boyfriend or the life I wanted to have because no one could love someone who looks like this."

Healthier thought: ....

STEP 4: LIVE A BALANCED LIFE

Once you're in recovery, you will need to restructure your life around the things that you value and love rather than around your symptoms. Check any of the following that you'd like to focus on and then add a few of your own.

☐ Hanging out with friends more.
☐ Doing things that you enjoy and that make you feel good about yourself.
☐ Dating.
☐ Getting a job or volunteering.
☐ Getting enough sleep on a normal day/night schedule.
☐ Eating well and getting enough exercise.
☐ Going to the doctor for regular check-ups to stay healthy or deal with any health problems that arise.

☐ ....

☐ ....

☐ ....

☐ ....

WEEK 10 ACTION STEPS

1. Plan for accountability by setting a day and time to check in with your support team each week to review the prior week and set goals for the coming week.
2. Create a reward plan for this week, and then update it weekly after you set your goals for the week with your support team.
3. Plan for setbacks by determining what you will do when they occur to keep them from turning into a relapse.

MY NEW REWARD PLAN

If I use . . . . strategies per . . . . (day or week) then I will earn: . . . .

Strategy	Mon	Tue	Wed	Thu	Fri	Sat	Sun

Congratulations, you have completed this workbook. I hope you are really proud of yourself for getting this far. Even if you're not where you hoped you would be, by working as hard as you did to complete this work, you have proven that you have what it takes to be in long-term recovery from your BFRB. If you're not where you want to be right now, go back and redo the workbook again, or pick and choose the chapters that you think will be most helpful for you.

If you are where you wanted to be, then you can put this book away for now, but don't get rid of it. It's likely that you will have a setback and may want to review this work or redo it to get back on track. Remember, everyone has setbacks. Those who successfully stay in recovery from their BFRBs are the ones who forgive themselves for the "mistakes" that lead to the setback, and with kindness and support, they pick themselves right back up and choose a new strategy.

By completing this book, you've proven that you've got what it takes to do just that. So, congratulations on giving yourself the gift of getting to live your life without your BFRB holding you back.

Resources

- The Picking Me Foundation: https://pickingme.org (or scan the QR code below)

- The Center for Mindfulness & CBT Online Courses: www.mindfulstlonline.com
- Overcoming Skin Picking and Hair Pulling: Help for BFRBs Facebook Group: www.facebook.com/groups/helpforbfrbs
- The TLC Foundation for Body-Focused Repetitive Behaviors: www.bfrb.org
- BFRB Changemakers: https://bfrbchangemakers.org
- BFRB UK & Ireland: www.bfrbukireland.com
- The Lyder Foundation for BFRBs: www.instagram.com/thelyderfoundation
- The International OCD Foundation: https://iocdf.org
- The Center for Mindfulness & CBT (for those in the St. Louis area): https://mindfulstl.com